Finding the Roots of Christianity

Finding the Roots of Christianity

A Spiritual and Historical Journey

LUKE PAINTER

RESOURCE *Publications* · Eugene, Oregon

FINDING THE ROOTS OF CHRISTIANITY
A Spiritual and Historical Journey

Resource Publications
An Imprint of Wipf and Stock Publishers
199 W. 8th Ave., Suite 3
Eugene, OR 97401

www.wipfandstock.com

PAPERBACK ISBN: 978-1-5326-0171-2
HARDCOVER ISBN: 978-1-5326-1031-8
EBOOK ISBN: 978-1-5326-1030-1

Manufactured in the U.S.A.   MAY 17, 2017

Block quotations from the Bible are from the Revised Standard Version (RSV), copyright 1952, 1971, Division of Christian Education of the National Council of the Churches of Christ in the United States of America. Shorter quotations are the author's own update of the King James Version and the RSV.

To my parents, who started me on this path.

"Make love your goal"

—Paul the apostle (1 Cor. 14:1)

Contents

Preface

Like many people who grew up with Christianity, I thought I knew who Jesus was and what the Bible was about. As I dug deeper, I began to peel back the layers of interpretation and tradition to see a different time and culture. I wanted to know who Jesus and his followers were in their own time and understanding, all those centuries ago. I tried to find out where the Bible came from and how it came to be the special book that it is today.

This book begins with an explanation of how I came to this subject, followed by some basic information, and discussion of some issues that arise from a historical study of Jesus and the New Testament. The latter part of the book explores sources relevant to understanding the origins of Christianity, including early Christian documents outside of the New Testament, and the writings of the Jewish historian Josephus. The rift between Jewish and non-Jewish Christians is discussed, as well as the transition of Christianity from obscure Jewish sect to the dominant religion of the Roman Empire.

I intended this to be a book that would have helped me as I began investigating these things, with a concise introduction to Christian historical origins, from a perspective of personal experience with religious faith. I hope the result will serve anyone with an interest in this subject, whether familiar with the Bible or not, and that in some small way the inspiration that drove me to write it will inspire the readers. So far, this book has been the source of some great conversations, a trend that I hope will continue.

Acknowledgments

I am grateful to friends who read early drafts of this book and offered helpful comments, including Ruth Watanabe, Bruce Johnston, Carter Kemp, Scott Stevenson, Mindy Vanderford, Walter Reece, Dave Borbridge, John Cunyus, Lenora O'Toole, and Richard Wallace. Elaine Pagels responded generously to my request that she review my manuscript, and I am grateful for her help and encouragement. I thank my parents, Joan and Robert Painter, for their support and suggestions. My mother volunteered to be my editor and her assistance greatly improved the outcome.

Abbreviations of Books of the Bible and Other Ancient Sources

HEBREW BIBLE (OLD TESTAMENT)

Gen	Genesis	Song	Song of Solomon
Exod	Exodus	Isa	Isaiah
Lev	Leviticus	Jer	Jeremiah
Num	Numbers	Lam	Lamentations
Deut	Deuteronomy	Ezek	Ezekiel
Josh	Joshua	Dan	Daniel
Judg	Judges	Hos	Hosea
Ruth	Ruth	Joel	Joel
1–2 Sam	1–2 Samuel	Amos	Amos
1–2 Kgs	1–2 Kings	Obad	Obadiah
1–2 Chr	1–2 Chronicles	Jonah	Jonah
Ezra	Ezra	Mic	Micah
Neh	Nehemiah	Nah	Nahum
Esth	Esther	Hab	Habbakuk
Job	Job	Zeph	Zephaniah
Ps	Psalms	Hag	Haggai
Prov	Proverbs	Zech	Zechariah
Eccl	Ecclesiastes	Mal	Malachi

ABBREVIATIONS OF BOOKS OF THE BIBLE

NEW TESTAMENT

Matt	Matthew	1–2 Thess	1–2 Thessalonians
Mark	Mark	1–2 Tim	1–2 Timothy
Luke	Luke	Titus	Titus
John	John	Phlm	Philemon
Acts	Acts of the Apostles	Heb	Hebrews
Rom	Romans	Jas	James
1–2 Cor	1–2 Corinthians	1–2 Pet	1–2 Peter
Gal	Galatians	1-2-3 John	1-2-3 John
Eph	Ephesians	Jude	Jude
Phil	Philippians	Rev	Revelation of John
Col	Colossians		

WRITINGS OF FLAVIUS JOSEPHUS

Antiquities	Antiquities of the Jews
War	The Jewish War
Life	Life of Flavius Josephus

OTHER EARLY CHRISTIAN TEXTS

Thomas	Gospel of Thomas
Didache	Didache (Teaching of the Twelve Apostles)

1

Belief and History

This is the story of my investigation of my Christian faith, and some interesting things I discovered. I hope it will be helpful to people who are curious about the Bible and Christianity and where it all came from. What does the evidence of history reveal about Jesus and his disciples and their followers, about who they were and what they thought? Historical sources can provide context for the life of Jesus, to understand him and the New Testament authors as people within their own culture and time. Documents outside the Bible can illuminate the world in which Christianity was born; however, the most important source is the Bible itself. The Bible is a religious document at the center of a major religion, but the search for the facts of history requires understanding the Bible as a historical document. I first became interested in the origins of Christianity as a result of my religious faith, but my exploration led to a much wider study of the culture and history of Jesus and his followers.

As a child I believed in traditional Christianity because my parents and other mentors and friends believed. I looked to the Christian Bible as the source and authority to understand my faith. I accepted the Bible as literally true and infallible, as do millions of Christians around the world. Membership in the community of believers became part of my identity, and this was a powerful influence on my early life. I sought my own relationship with God, as did people in the Bible and in my church. I felt obligated to defend the doctrines of my religion, and had some trepidation when I began questioning them. The Bible was a friend and source of daily inspiration, and this made it difficult to question the idea that it is perfect.

Biblical infallibility or inerrancy may seem a strange idea in the modern world, but for many Christians it is a fundamental doctrine. Belief in the Christian Bible as the one infallible authority is a unifying principle among evangelical Christians, tying together a vast community of people from several major denominations and many independent churches. One such large and venerated organization is the Southern Baptist Convention, which states as a basic belief that, "The Holy Bible was written by men divinely inspired and is God's revelation of Himself to man. It is a perfect treasure of divine instruction. It has God for its author, salvation for its end, and truth, without any mixture of error, for its matter. Therefore, all Scripture is totally true and trustworthy."[1] If this is true, it certainly simplifies the search for historical facts about Jesus and the early Christians! I could start by simply accepting that everything the Bible says is literally true and factual. Setting aside the lens of religious belief, it is clear that the Bible is unlikely to be perfect and infallible, because it was written by humans and nothing done by humans is infallible. Nevertheless, this is the standard to which millions of people hold the Bible. How can so many people accept such a radical belief?

People may simply accept belief in the perfection of the Bible as part of the package of their religion, but for many believers the Bible also has the power to inspire faith in God. From this follows reverence for the Bible, and from this reverence follows the conviction that everything in it must be true and right. I had spiritual experiences that reinforced and internalized my belief in God, and I interpreted these experiences in light of my religious training and the Bible.

Most spiritual experiences are difficult to explain to another person, but I can relate an experience that strengthened my belief in the Bible. It happened when I was twelve years old. I was sitting alone under some trees, with some things on my mind, fretting more than thinking. I looked up at the sky, and I heard a voice loud and clear, saying, "My son, rest in me. Be still and know that I am God." I believed it was the voice of God. I was astounded and my worries shattered.

The voice was clear, but I cannot say that someone else sitting there would have heard it, maybe it was in my mind. I already believed in God and was studying the Bible. I knew part of this was from Psalm 46:10, "Be still and know that I am God," but what really hit me was the love behind it, the loving God who called me son and wanted me to be at peace. This

---

1. Southern Baptist Convention, *Basic Beliefs*.

confirmed and strengthened my belief in God, and in the Bible as the infallible Word of God. I cultivated a sense of the presence of God, and listened for the still, small, voice of the Holy Spirit.

This kind of experience has consequences for the way a person reads the Bible. For example, the Bible says that Jesus had a similar experience when he was baptized by John the Baptist:

> When he came up out of the water, immediately he saw the heavens opened and the Spirit descending upon him like a dove; and a voice came from heaven, "You are my beloved son, with you I am well pleased." (Mark 1:10–11)[2]

Historians often discount such miraculous occurrences in the Bible as nonfactual legends, but for me it was easy to believe that Jesus and others in the Bible had experiences like this, because something similar happened to me. When people questioned the Bible, it seemed to me they did not understand that it came from the living Spirit of God. For my parents, who were church pastors, the skepticism they had encountered in their seminary training seemed to take the faith and life out of the Bible. We found ourselves identifying with the Christians of the New Testament, as we sought and experienced the reality of God. The important thing, we thought, was for people to believe in the living Holy Spirit. This brought real and tangible benefits to their lives, so questioning the Bible seemed counterproductive. There appeared to be only two ways to go: believing in God and the Holy Spirit and the perfection of the Bible, or rejecting the whole thing. I later came to realize there is another option, but that stark choice was how it looked to me then.

As I grew older, I felt a responsibility to myself, God, and the truth to question beliefs I had accepted uncritically. I wanted to truly understand the Bible and Christianity, and I wanted my faith to be grounded in truth. I believed that any real God would want me to use reason and wisdom. I had a sense of God's presence that affirmed "God is love," as the Bible says (1 John 4:8), a simple phrase that for me conveyed a reality beyond words. Jesus said that loving God and loving your neighbor fulfills God's purpose (Matt. 7:12, 22:37–40). He told his disciples, "This is my commandment that you love one another" (John 15:12). I believed in this heart of love and forgiveness, but set aside the traditional doctrines of Christianity. I believed in God but recognized that this belief cannot be objectively proven.

---

2. Citations from the Bible are provided in the text using abbreviations for the books of the Bible.

I cannot prove that compassion and kindness are keys to a good life, but this is something anyone can practice regardless of their beliefs. There are compassionate people who are not religious and do not believe in God, and there are hateful people who are very religious and seem to genuinely believe in God. Jesus said it is their actions that show his true followers, not their vows of allegiance (Matt. 7:15–23), and people who are loving and kind are serving God whether they know it or not (Matt. 25:31–46). His followers are to serve one another in love and humility (Mark 9:35, John 13:14). To have your sins forgiven, simply forgive the sins of others (Matt. 5:14–15). In these teachings of Jesus I saw the same Spirit that inspired me, and it was through the Bible, perfect or not, that I came to this. Because the Bible was important to me personally, I wanted to know what it was and how it came to be written. Furthermore, the writings of the Bible and related ancient documents contain the most important historical evidence available for the origins of Christianity, a movement that has influenced the lives of many people and the history of the world.

2

The Bible and the Story of Jesus

How can the Bible be understood as a historical source? The most direct way is to examine what it says. The New Testament of the Bible contains almost everything known about Jesus and the early beginnings of Christianity, including letters written by the apostle Paul, one of Christianity's important founders. For centuries, Christians have looked to these writings as authoritative and inspired by God. A careful study will reveal the humanity of the Bible authors, as people within a time and culture. Some of the conclusions from this investigation may seem radical to someone who has heard only the traditional religious point of view, but familiar to anyone with an introductory course on the New Testament from a college or seminary.

Jesus and his disciples were Jews in the land of Israel, which was at that time, 2000 years ago, under the control of the vast and powerful Roman Empire. As observant Jews they followed Jewish ritual practices and dietary laws, avoided work on the Sabbath day, and revered a set of scriptures that later were adopted as the Old Testament of the Christian Bible. These ancient Jewish writings are an important source for understanding not only ancient Judaism but also Jesus and his disciples and their followers, who were the source and the subject of the second part of the Christian Bible called the New Testament. The Bible, therefore, has two parts: the Old Testament containing the holy scriptures of the Jews, originally written in Hebrew; and the New Testament, written in Greek, containing the oldest and most revered documents of Christianity. The writings of the Bible were produced by various authors and editors over a span of centuries, and had no chapter or verse divisions in their original form.

The Jewish temple in the city of Jerusalem was the heart of the Jewish world and culture. Jews believed that the spirit of almighty God resided there, in the Holy of Holies, the inner court of the temple. Priests in the temple performed rituals prescribed by the Jewish laws, including animal sacrifices. There were annual holy days when many thousands of people gathered in Jerusalem, and the biggest of these was the Passover. A similar event in the world today is the Muslim Hajj, the annual pilgrimage to Mecca where thousands of pilgrims perform ancient rituals that include sacrificing an animal. At the time of Jesus, many Jews made an annual pilgrimage to Jerusalem for the Passover holy day, which involved a ritual feast. For this meal they ate a lamb, sacrificed by priests in the temple. Other sacrifices were done for other purposes, and there were people in the temple courtyard selling animals for sacrifices. The temple was controlled by priests from the sect of the Sadducees, who usually worked independently of the Romans but were under the authority of the Roman governor.[1]

The story of Jesus of Nazareth is told in four different books called the four Gospels: the Gospel according to Matthew, Mark, Luke and John. These were written in Greek, the common language of the Mediterranean world at that time, and are collected in the New Testament along with other early Christian writings. The word "gospel" (Greek *evangelion*) originally meant a message, proclamation, or good news, and this is what Christians called their message of Jesus the Christ.[2] I will use "Gospels" capitalized to refer to the four accounts of Jesus in the Bible. Three of the four—Matthew, Mark, and Luke—are called the "synoptic" Gospels because they are much more similar to each other than the fourth, John.

No one knows who actually wrote these books that tell the story of Jesus. The earliest versions apparently were anonymous, with titles added later to reflect traditions about who may have written them.[3] For brevity, I will refer to the unknown authors of these books by their traditional names. They all tell the same basic story: Jesus of Nazareth was a prophet, healer, worker of miracles, and teacher of righteousness who proclaimed the Kingdom of Heaven on earth. A prophet was one who had a special connection with God and spoke a message from God, while a teacher or

---

1. Schiffman, *Understanding Second Temple and Rabbinic Judaism* ch. 5; Newsome, *Greeks, Romans, Jews,* ch. 9.

2. Harris, *New Testament,* 7–8; Koester, *Ancient Christian Gospels.*

3. See any good introduction to New Testament history. For most of the basic history of the gospels I relied on Harris, *New Testament*; Ehrman, *Jesus: Apocalyptic Prophet*; Ehrman, *New Testament*; Pagels, *Beyond Belief.*

rabbi interpreted the scriptures and traditions to apply them in life. More than that, according to the Gospels, Jesus was the Jewish Messiah, called "Christ" (*christos*) in Greek, a savior from God whom many Jews expected would come soon to free them from oppression and restore the nation of Israel. The Messiah or Christ literally meant the anointed one, referring to the practice of anointing the head of a king or priest with oil as a sign of their special position (1 Sam. 10:1, for example). The Messiah would bring peace, prosperity and righteousness—the Kingdom of Heaven on earth. Some Jews looked for restoration of the past glories of Israel under the legendary King David, but many believed that "the Day of the Lord" would involve a miraculous transformation of the world, and the resurrection of the dead.[4] Jesus, at about thirty years of age, gathered a following, then was arrested by the Jewish authorities and crucified by the Romans, about the year 30 CE.[5] According to the Gospel accounts he was resurrected and exalted by God, proving that he really was the Messiah or Christ, and the Kingdom of Heaven really was at hand as he said. These four "Gospels" are the starting point for understanding Christianity.

Differences between the four Gospels provide clues to the relationships between them. An example is the story of Jesus causing a disruption in the temple, traditionally called "cleansing the temple," an event that may have precipitated his arrest and execution. Jesus and many other devout Jews did not approve of the way the temple was operated,[6] and Jesus apparently objected to something about the business of selling the sacrificial animals in the temple. He created a disturbance and disrupted the temple business to make his point that the temple "should be a house of prayer . . . but you have made it a den of thieves" (Mark 11:17). In the four Gospels, there are two different versions of when and how Jesus did this dramatic prophetic act. One version places this event at the end of his ministry, the other at the beginning.

In the three synoptic Gospels (Matthew, Mark, and Luke), this disruption in the temple was the final confrontation that led to the arrest of Jesus,

---

4. Newsome, *Greeks, Romans, Jews*, ch. 3; Schiffman, *Reclaiming the Dead Sea Scrolls*, ch. 19; Levine, *Misunderstood Jew*, ch. 1, 2, 4.

5. CE (for Common Era) is the international equivalent of the older designation AD, counting from the traditional year of the birth of Christ. Dates before this are labeled "BCE." Historians now date the death of Herod the Great at 4 BCE, so Jesus must have been born by that time if he was born during Herod's reign, as both Matthew and Luke attest.

6. Schiffman. *Qumran and Jerusalem*, ch. 4; Levine, *Misunderstood Jew*, ch. 4.

the culmination of growing tensions between Jesus and Jewish authorities who feared he would gain a large following (Mark 11:18). In contrast, in the Gospel of John the temple disruption was almost the first thing Jesus did, setting the stage for his prophetic activities, as if announcing his intentions right from the start (John 2:13–15). Then a few years later he was arrested for his growing fame and influence after raising Lazarus from the dead (John 11). This discrepancy is easy to explain if the gospels are a collection of stories passed around orally and finally written down by different people. The temple disturbance was known to be part of the story, as was the arrest of Jesus, but the author of John followed a different timeline and a different explanation for the arrest.

I once thought that Jesus must have disrupted the temple twice, combining the two stories, but there is little room for this in either version. Combining them distorts what the Gospels actually say, making a new story rather than taking them at their word. In addition, John's accounts of the crucifixion and resurrection of Jesus are incompatible with the other Gospels, at least in the details. Readers of the Bible often assume that John was aware of the other Gospels and supplementing them, but these discrepancies suggest that this author either did not know the other versions, or did not agree with them, a clue to understanding the Gospels as historical documents. These observations are nothing new; the influential third century theologian Origen pointed out differences between the Gospels, and proposed that the Gospels should be interpreted mystically or symbolically, since they are not always factually consistent.[7]

Another well-known event in the life of Jesus is his birth, celebrated at Christmas. Most people are unaware of the fact that the two versions of the Christmas story (from Matthew and Luke) are inconsistent with each other. I did not notice this until it was pointed out to me, because I would always read Matthew with Luke in mind, assuming they were the same. Reading the two accounts with an open mind, it is easy to see the basic differences. The familiar story is told in the Gospel of Luke, of Mary and Joseph who lived in Nazareth (Luke 1:26, 2:39). They traveled to Bethlehem where Jesus was born in a stable (because there was no room in the inn). They were visited by shepherds, then returned to Nazareth where Jesus grew up. This is the story often told at Christmas.

---

7. Origen, *Commentary on John* 10:1–16; Pagels, *Beyond Belief*, 37, 118; for the works of Origen see Kirby, *Early Christian Writings*.

The story is different in the Gospel of Matthew. In this version, Mary and Joseph lived in Bethlehem (not Nazareth) when Jesus was born there (Matt. 2). They remained there until after the visit by the "wise men," astrologers who saw his star when he was born and later found Mary and Jesus in their house (not an inn or stable) in Bethlehem. Jesus may have been born about two years prior to the visit of the wise men, because King Herod the Great (King of the Jews under the Romans) ordered the murder of all male children younger than two years in Bethlehem, based on when the astrologers told him the star had appeared. Warned in a dream, Joseph took the family to Egypt to escape King Herod. He intended to return to Bethlehem after the death of Herod, but it was still too dangerous so they settled in Nazareth where Jesus grew up (Matt. 2:19–23).

It is clear from elsewhere in the four Gospels that Matthew and Luke were aware of a problem: Jesus was known to be from the town of Nazareth in the province of Galilee (Mark 1:9, John 1:46, for example), but the Messiah was supposed to be from Bethlehem, the city of David, according to an Old Testament prophecy (Matt. 2:5, John 7:41–52). Christians said Jesus of Nazareth was this Messiah, but he was not from Bethlehem. Matthew and Luke solved this problem by reporting that Jesus was born in Bethlehem then grew up in Nazareth, but each author had a different version of how this happened. They also knew that the Messiah was expected to be a descendant of David, and provided genealogies to prove this, but the genealogies are incompatible (Matt. 1, Luke 3).[8] The two birth stories are contradictory in their details, but they make the same main point: Jesus is the Christ, foretold by the prophets. As with the story of Jesus disrupting the temple, these discrepancies show that each writer either was unaware of the other version or did not agree with it. These conflicting Christmas stories demonstrate that to really understand the Bible it is necessary to allow it to be inconsistent, taking the writers on their own terms. Otherwise, I may end up trying to force Matthew to tell Luke's story and miss what Matthew was actually intending to say.

As with the birth story, the accounts of the resurrection of Jesus are revealing about the nature of the Bible and its relationship to the historical events on which it is based. It is impossible to harmonize the details of the five different resurrection accounts (four Gospels, plus 1 Cor. 15:3–8). The

---

8. People sometimes say that one genealogy is through the mother line and the other through the father, but there is no way to completely reconcile them, as comparing them will show.

four Gospels generally agree that there was an empty tomb and later some people saw Jesus, but they have different versions of who went to the tomb, what they saw there, who saw Jesus first, what Jesus or angels or a young man said to them, and how the disciples reacted. At least some of the details are incompatible. This is what would be expected if the Gospels came from stories that were passed around orally and later written down by various people.

A similar example is the question of how Judas Iscariot died, and what happened to the money he got for betraying Jesus. Most people familiar with the story would remember that he hung himself after throwing the money down in front of the priests, as related in the Gospel of Matthew (27:3–10). However, the Acts of the Apostles (1:15) has a strange and different version, in which Judas bought a field with the money and later fell to his death there. The only thing the two stories have in common is that his body ended up in a place called the Field of Blood. This is easy to understand if people thought Judas was buried in this place, and different oral traditions developed about how this happened and why it was called the Field of Blood. At least one of these stories must be wrong in its details, and again it is clear that the writers did not agree with each other.

The Gospels also disagree about the day on which Jesus was arrested and crucified. Was it the day of the Passover holy day (as in the synoptic Gospels) or the day before Passover (as in John)? According to the synoptic Gospels, Jesus ate the Passover evening meal with his disciples (the famous Last Supper). Using the ritual bread and wine, he asked them to add a new meaning to the ancient ritual as a memorial to him (this became the Christian Eucharist or Lord's Supper). He was arrested later that night and crucified the next morning. This was still the Passover day since Jewish days start at sundown. Mark (14:12) describes the day of preparation for the Passover: " . . . the first day of unleavened bread, when they sacrificed the Passover lamb, his disciples said to him, 'Where will you have us go and prepare for you to eat the Passover?'" Later that evening they ate the Passover feast, and then Jesus was crucified the next morning "at the third hour" (Mark 15:25). Therefore, the Last Supper was the Passover supper, and Jesus was crucified the next morning during the day of Passover. This is the timing most Christians have traditionally accepted.

In the Gospel of John, "before the feast of the Passover," they had supper and Jesus washed the disciples' feet (John 13:1). This was the Last Supper. Then Jesus was arrested and taken to the High Priest Caiaphas (John

18), who early the next morning took him to the Roman governor Pilate, but John 18:28 says: "they themselves [Caiaphas and the priests] did not enter into the praetorium [Roman judgment hall], so that they would not be defiled; but would be able to eat the Passover." They had not yet eaten the Passover feast! John makes the timing very clear, as Jesus is sentenced to death: "It was the day of Preparation of the Passover; it was about the sixth hour" (John 19:14). It was one day earlier than in Mark, and three hours later in the day. John 19:31 tells us again: "it was the day of preparation [for the Passover]." According to the Gospel of John, Jesus had his last supper with the disciples the evening before the Passover, and was crucified on the day of preparation for the Passover feast.[9] His last supper was the day before the Passover.

Having discovered that John disagrees with the other Gospels about whether or not the Last Supper was the Passover, what does this mean? As with the other examples, it demonstrates that some of the details of the Gospel accounts are not consistent. This makes sense if the Bible was written and compiled after a time of passing these stories around. Different accounts would come from different people, and they might not get all the facts straight. Also, some details may change as the story is retold over and over by different people. Looking deeper, a clue may be in John 1:29 where Jesus is described as "the Lamb of God, who takes away the sin of the world." Jesus was literally sacrificed as the Lamb of God at the same time the lambs were sacrificed for the Passover! The symbolism of Jesus as the sacrifice lamb emphasizes the message of the Gospel of John, but may have biased the way the story was told, changing the timing of events.

Alternatively, there are good reasons to think John's timeline might be the correct one. For one thing, it seems very unlikely that the priests involved in the arrest and trial would have been willing to do these things on the high and holy Passover day. All such work was forbidden, especially for priests. It is easy to imagine early Jewish Christians combining the new memorial ritual about Jesus with the traditional Passover, and losing the detail that the Last Supper was actually the day before. Either way, by recognizing this inconsistency I am better able to understand what the scriptures literally say in their own words.

---

9. For further discussion see: Ehrman, *New Testament*, 55–57; Harris, *New Testament*, 191–92; Sanders, *Historical Figure of Jesus*; Pagels, *Beyond Belief*, 35–37; Levine, *Misunderstood Jew*, 207–10.

Even with these differences the basic message of the Gospels is much the same: Jesus is the Christ, the Jewish Messiah, the Son of God, the Savior who brings the Kingdom of Heaven. It is also clear that even knowing the facts of the Bible, I still do not have a clear view of Jesus. Some of the details in the Bible stories are contradictory and have been embellished through retelling, so it is difficult or impossible to tell what actually happened in detail. Therefore, the entire picture must remain a little fuzzy. If anyone doubts that the New Testament has internal contradictions, I suggest they read the four Gospel accounts of the resurrection of Jesus, and jot down a basic timeline of events for each—who went where and did what, and what they saw and heard. Then try to find a believable way to reconcile these details. When I first tried this exercise as a teenager, I fully expected every-thing to fit together like a puzzle, but found the pieces were not compatible. This made sense when I realized that the New Testament was written by people who, like me, were fallible; people who believed they had something important to communicate. Who were these people and what was their message?

3

According to the Scriptures

THE WORD OF GOD

The followers of Jesus and his disciples, who were Jews, based their message about Jesus on concepts and prophecies from the Jewish scriptures, which they believed to be inspired by God. These scriptures often expressed reverence for the word of God, referring to the Law of Moses, called the Torah or Pentateuch, the first five books of the Bible. A familiar example is Psalm 119:105: "Thy word is a lamp to my feet, and a light to my path." According to tradition, the great Jewish prophet Moses wrote these five books, and the commandments in them were actually written by God on tablets of stone (Exo. 34). By the time of Jesus, most Jews accepted as inspired a collection of books called "the Law and the prophets," which included the Torah (the Law) plus additional books attributed to prophets, and also the book of Psalms and some other historical and literary writings. This collection of Jewish scriptures was later adopted by Christians as the Old Testament of the Christian Bible.

When the writers of the New Testament referred to sacred scriptures, these Jewish scriptures were what they had in mind. For example, in the Gospels, Jesus prefaced some of his statements with "It is written . . . " and then quoted an Old Testament passage (Matt. 4:4–10). Jesus said he had come to fulfill "the Law and the prophets" (Matt. 5:17).

A well-known reference to the Old Testament scriptures is found in the Second Epistle to Timothy:

> . . . from childhood you have been acquainted with the sacred
> writings which are able to instruct you for salvation through faith

13

> in Christ Jesus. All scripture is inspired by God and profitable for
> teaching, for reproof, for correction, and for training in righteous-
> ness, that the man of God may be complete, equipped for every
> good work. (2 Tim. 3:15–16, RSV)

It is clear from the context that this verse was referring to the Jewish Bible,
the books of the Old Testament, which this writer believed were inspired
by God. As this verse states, Christians believed that the Jewish scriptures
foretold God's plan of salvation through Jesus, who was the Christ. The
apostle Paul expressed this belief when he wrote that Jesus died "in accordance with the scriptures" and was raised "in accordance with the scriptures" (1 Cor. 15:3).

In contrast to the Old Testament, in the New Testament many references to the "word of God" or "the word" are not about scriptures at all,
but about spoken words. These passages use the Greek word *logos*, which
means the living or spoken word, or a teaching or message. This is the same
word used in the Gospel of John to describe Jesus as "the word of God" who
made all things (John 1). This idea of the divine word of creation was used
by some ancient Greek philosophers, and appears in the story of creation in
the Jewish scriptures, when God speaks the world into existence (Gen. 1).[1]
Most of the time, however, "the word" (*logos*) had the simple meaning of a
spoken message, as in these examples from the New Testament:

- "the word of truth, the gospel of your salvation" (Eph. 1:13)
- "the implanted word, which is able to save your souls" (Jas. 1:21);
- "rightly dividing the word of truth" (2 Tim. 2:15);
- "the word of God is quick, and powerful, and sharper than any two-
  edged sword" (Heb. 4:12);
- "unskilled in the word of righteousness" (Heb. 6:13);
- "as babes, desire the sincere milk of the word" (Greek *logikos*, verbal
  reasoning, teaching, 1 Pet. 2:2).

These passages emphasize the teaching and preaching of the gospel
message, person to person. Preaching and persuasion were important,
because the Jewish scriptures alone were not enough to convince people
to accept the Christian interpretation of those scriptures. To most Jews,

---

1. Newsome, *Greeks, Romans, Jews*, 237, 369; Barrett, *New Testament Background*
262–64; on the use of *logos* in John, see Levine and Brettler, *Jewish Annotated New Testament* 546–48.

Jesus clearly was not the Christ. He had been killed by the Romans and had not restored the independence and power of Israel, which was what they expected the Christ or Messiah to do at a minimum. The hope of a triumphant savior is demonstrated by a famous passage from the prophet Isaiah that was thought to be a prophecy of the Messiah:

> For to us a child is born, to us a son is given; and the government will be upon his shoulder, and his name will be called "Wonderful Counselor, Mighty God, Everlasting Father, Prince of Peace." Of the increase of his government and of peace there will be no end, upon the throne of David, and over his kingdom, to establish it, and to uphold it with justice and with righteousness from this time forth and for evermore. The zeal of the Lord of hosts will do this. (Isa. 9:6–7, RSV)

This expectation of the Messiah and the Christian response to it are illustrated by a story in the Gospel of Luke that took place after the crucifixion and resurrection of Jesus. Two followers of Jesus walking on a road were joined by the resurrected Jesus, but they did not recognize him. They told him they were discussing recent events concerning Jesus of Nazareth, "a prophet mighty in word and deed," and they "had hoped he was the one to redeem Israel," but he had been crucified (Luke 24:21). They had given up hope, but some of the women said he was not in his tomb and had seen angels saying he was still alive. Still unrecognized, Jesus berated them for their unbelief, saying "O foolish men, and slow of heart to believe all that the prophets have spoken! Was it not necessary that the Christ should suffer these things and enter into his glory?" Then, "beginning with Moses and all the prophets, he interpreted to them in the scriptures the things concerning himself." Later they recognized him and he vanished; then they said to each other, "Did not our hearts burn within us while he talked to us on the road, while he opened to us the scriptures?" (Luke 24:25–32). The suggestion is that they should have known—after all, it was in the Jewish scriptures.

This story demonstrates how the followers of Jesus addressed the question of Jesus as the Christ. They had thought he was the new King and Messiah to restore Israel, but their hopes were dashed when he was crucified. Then, they came to believe he was resurrected and was the Messiah after all, and this changed their understanding of what the Messiah was intended to do. They revised the meaning of the Messiah, and reinterpreted the Jewish scriptures to support this new meaning.

As the story continues, the two disciples who saw Jesus on the road arrived in Jerusalem and related their experience to the other disciples. Jesus suddenly appeared among them, and said:

> "These are my words which I spoke to you, while I was still with you, that everything written about me in the law of Moses and the prophets and the psalms must be fulfilled." Then he opened their minds to understand the scriptures, and said to them, "Thus it is written, that the Christ should suffer and on the third day rise from the dead, and that repentance and forgiveness of sins should be preached in his name to all nations, beginning from Jerusalem. You are witnesses of these things." (Luke 24:44–47, RSV)

According to this account, Jesus himself (after his resurrection) explained to his disciples how the Jewish scriptures had foretold these events. Christians said the crucifixion of Jesus was all part of God's plan, prophesied in the scriptures (see John 5:39–47, Acts 8:26–39). His resurrection proved that the change had already started.

There is no evidence in any non-Christian Jewish writings that this belief in a Messiah who was to suffer, and be rejected and killed, was ever held by anyone except Christians, who adopted it in hindsight. Passages such as Psalm 22 and Isaiah 53 from the Old Testament were interpreted by Christians as prophesies of a suffering Christ, but there is no evidence that these were understood as Messianic prophesies by other Jews of the time.[2] This argument over the meaning of the Messiah, and the claim that the Christian version was prophesied in the Old Testament, are threads that run throughout the New Testament. It was written primarily by Christian Jews who believed they were the true followers of the Jewish God and his Messiah. This is a major theme in the four Gospels and in the letters of Paul, who reinterpreted Judaism to fit his new understanding of God's plan and of Jesus as the Christ.

FULFILLING THE WORDS OF THE PROPHETS

It is a fact of history that most Jews did not accept the Christian interpretation of the Jewish scriptures. Even today, Orthodox Jews await the Messiah, and utterly reject the Christian interpretation of their holy scriptures. However, many Jews of Jesus' time agreed with the basic approach of finding

---

2. Ben Witherington III, "Isaiah 53:1–12 (Septuagint)," ch. 27 in Levine et al., *Historical Jesus*; Ehrman, *New Testament*, 279–80; Levine, *Misunderstood Jew*, 209–11.

scriptures to support their claims, even if the scriptures were out of context. There was a common belief that the holy scriptures contained hidden prophetic meanings that could be understood by a person with special insight, or at the right time. This kind of thinking pervades the New Testament, as well as other early Christian[3] and Jewish writings of the time such as the Dead Sea Scrolls.[4] It is a mystical, allegorical, revelation-based way of interpreting scriptures, not the way most people today think of prophecy. In this way of thinking it is the secret hidden meaning that matters, not what the prophet actually was talking about or understood the message to mean. This approach could extend to long passages, as in the Dead Sea Scrolls where books from the Old Testament such as Habakkuk were interpreted allegorically to give them a new meaning for a later time. Similarly, the philosopher Philo of Alexandria (a contemporary of Jesus) wrote a commentary on the Torah that interpreted the Jewish laws and scriptures allegorically.[5] Later, Christians also wrote allegorical interpretations of the Old Testament, such as the Epistle of Barnabas. This book, included in some early versions of the New Testament, said Jews were mistaken to interpret their laws and scriptures literally because the true meaning was allegorical.[6]

The theme of Jesus the Christ as the fulfillment of Jewish scripture was important to early Christians, and the author of the Gospel of Matthew was particularly interested in prophecies of Jesus, with five examples in just the first two chapters. It is instructive to consider these examples of prophecy fulfillment in greater depth. In the story of the birth of Jesus in Matthew, after Joseph finds out that Mary is pregnant by the Holy Spirit, the author comments:

> All this took place to fulfill what the Lord had spoken by the prophet: "Behold, a virgin shall conceive and bear a son, and his name shall be called Emmanuel" (which means, God with us). (Matt. 1:22–23, RSV)

In this passage, the author of the Gospel of Matthew quoted Isaiah (7:14), the Old Testament prophet. There are two well-known difficulties with this passage, and each reveals something about the way Matthew used

---

3. Ehrman, *Orthodox Corruption of Scripture* 20–22.

4. Ehrman, *New Testament*, 238; Newsome, *Greeks, Romans, Jews*, ch. 5; Schiffman, *Reclaiming the Dead Sea Scrolls*, ch. 14.

5. Newsome, *Greeks, Romans, Jews*, 368–72; Barrett, *New Testament Background*, ch. 10.

6. Ehrman, *Lost Scriptures*, 219–35.

scripture.[7] First, the context of the passage in Isaiah is clear, and it was not a prophecy of the Messiah in its original meaning. It was about a child who would be born in Isaiah's own time, as a sign from God that the enemies threatening Ahaz the King of Judah would not succeed (Isaiah 7:18). There is no evidence that other Jews of Jesus' time saw this verse as predicting the Messiah, and Matthew was the only New Testament author to cite this verse. This reading may be Matthew's innovation, and is not consistent with the original meaning or the way the verse was normally interpreted.

Second, this Old Testament scripture (Isaiah 7:14) said nothing about the birth of this child being miraculous, and did not use the word "virgin" (Hebrew *bethulah*) in the original Hebrew. Instead, it simply said "a young woman" (Hebrew *almah*) will have a child, so "young woman" is the correct translation and makes sense in the original context. Matthew, like other Greek-speaking Jews of his time, used a Greek translation of the Hebrew scriptures called the Septuagint. Many Jews accepted this Greek translation as inspired and authoritative in every word, and it is the version of the Old Testament quoted in the New Testament by other authors as well as Matthew.[8] In Greek, the word (*parthenos*) used for the Hebrew "young woman" means a young woman who is unmarried and a virgin. Matthew's interpretation was based on the typical Greek meaning of the word, but this meaning was inconsistent with both its original context and the original Hebrew. It is as if someone were to base a fulfillment of prophecy on a meaning that is found only in an English translation of the Bible, but not in the original language. This was the way Matthew interpreted this Old Testament scripture.

Another use of hidden meanings in scripture is found in Matthew 2:15: "This was done to fulfill what the Lord had spoken by the prophet, 'Out of Egypt have I called my son.'" Recall that in Matthew's birth story, the family of Jesus fled to Egypt to avoid Herod, then later returned to Nazareth. Matthew quoted the prophet Hosea to show that this was a fulfillment of prophecy; here is the passage in its original context:

> . . . the tumult of war shall arise among your people, and all your fortresses shall be destroyed, as Shalman destroyed Betharbel on the day of battle; mothers were dashed in pieces with their children. Thus it shall be done to you, O house of Israel, because of

---

7. Harris, *New Testament*, 140; Levine and Brettler, *Jewish Annotated New Testament*, 4; Newsome, *Greeks, Romans, Jews*, ch. 6.

8. Ehrman, *New Testament*, 38; Levine, *Misunderstood Jew*, ch. 6.

your great wickedness. In the storm the king of Israel shall be utterly cut off. When Israel was a child, I loved him, and out of Egypt
I called my son. The more I called them, the more they went from
me; they kept sacrificing to the Baals, and burning incense to idols.
(Hos. 10:14—11:2, RSV)

The meaning of the original text is clear, and it is not about the Messiah at all. It is a familiar theme in the Old Testament: God mourning over
the people of Israel and the destruction that has come on them as a result
of worshiping other gods. The "son" is a reference to the children of Israel,
God's chosen people, and the passage is recalling the Exodus from Egypt,
when the nation of Israel was young, one of the most important events in
the relationship between God and his people. As with the passage from
Isaiah used to support the virgin birth, Matthew's interpretation of this
scripture was not consistent with the meaning of the passage in its original
context. Likewise, when Matthew quoted Jeremiah 31:15 (Matt. 2:17–18)
about "Rachel weeping for her children" his interpretation ignored the clear
meaning of the scripture in Jeremiah. It was not a prophecy of the future,
rather, it referred to the suffering and exile of Jews in Jeremiah's own time.

The birth narrative in the Gospel of Matthew concludes with another
miraculous fulfillment of prophecy, when Joseph and family settle in Nazareth. Matthew quoted a prophecy that "he shall be called a Nazarene" as
proof that the Jewish scriptures foretold the Messiah would come from
Nazareth (Matt. 2:23). Matthew seems to have been referring to the account
of the birth of Samson (Judg. 13:5). An angel told Samson's mother that the
boy would be a Nazarite, which means a man with a special dedication to
God, and who never cuts his hair or drinks strong drink. Matthew saw a
double meaning in the word Nazarite as a prophecy that the Messiah would
come from Nazareth. This interpretation is unique to the Gospel of Matthew and has no connection to the original meaning of the Old Testament
scripture that supposedly was being fulfilled.

It is clear that in most cases the author of the Gospel of Matthew did
not take Old Testament scriptures at their literal and obvious meaning in
context. He gave them an entirely new interpretation based on hidden
meanings and hindsight to make them apply to current events, a method
that was common in his time. This is not objective proof for Jesus as the
Messiah, as Christians claimed; rather, it relies on accepting Matthew's
novel and creative use of scriptures and their hidden meanings. As preachers today may take a verse out of context to make a point, or may read

current events into the Biblical text, Matthew manipulated Old Testament scriptures to show that Jesus fulfilled prophecy.

As mentioned previously, one prophecy on which Matthew, Luke and many of their contemporaries agreed was that the Messiah would be born in Bethlehem (Matt. 2:5, Luke 2:11, John 7:41–42). Matthew quoted the prophet Micah (5:2), who foretold the restoration of Israel and a time of peace and freedom from foreign enemies, through a ruler who would come from Bethlehem. Matthew and Luke wanted to show that Jesus actually was born in Bethlehem, to establish his credentials as the Messiah. Other New Testament writers handled the question of Jesus' hometown in different ways. The issue never comes up in the Gospel of Mark, which says nothing about the birth of Jesus, simply that he "came from Nazareth of Galilee" (Mark 1:9). Similarly, Paul wrote nothing about the birth of Jesus except that he was "born of a woman" (Gal. 4:4), that is, he was born like everybody else. The Gospel of John also has no mention of the birth of Jesus, except that "the word [*logos*, of God] became flesh and lived among us" (John 1:14). John identified Jesus as "Jesus of Nazareth, the son of Joseph" (John 1:45), and acknowledged that some people thought his hometown disqualified him from being the Messiah (John 7:40–52), but made no argument that he was really from Bethlehem. Only Matthew and Luke shared the concern to show that Jesus was born in Bethlehem, and that he was miraculously born of a virgin.

Given the absence of any mention of the virgin birth in the New Testament outside of Matthew and Luke, it seems clear that the virgin birth was not part of the original gospel message. If it were, Paul or Mark or John would have mentioned it, and John would not have identified Jesus simply as "the son of Joseph." Perhaps the virgin birth story was added to satisfy the desire for a miraculous birth story suitable for such an important and divine person. In Jewish tradition, important prophets and leaders often had miraculous births (Isaac, Moses, Samson and Samuel, for example), and for non-Jews the claim that Jesus was "the son of God" meant that some kind of divine intervention must have been involved in his birth. However, Paul and the other New Testament writers seem to have been unacquainted with these birth stories about Jesus and showed no interest in such questions. The virgin birth was not part of Paul, Mark or John's gospel message.

Although Paul did not share Matthew's interest in the birth of Jesus, he did share the tendency to look for texts in the Jewish scriptures to support his arguments, and Paul was willing to stretch the meaning to make his point (for example, Gal. 3:6–16).[9] Like Matthew, Paul believed the Christian message of Jesus as the Christ was "in accordance with the scriptures" (1 Cor. 15:3–4). Matthew and Paul used techniques of interpretation that were common in their time,[10] but their reading of scripture often was not based on what the scriptures actually meant in their original context. It was a mystical way of thinking that relied on interpretation by hindsight. Paul based his message on direct revelation that Jesus was the Christ, and this revelation was what he used to understand the hidden meaning of the Jewish scriptures (1 Cor. 2, Gal. 1).

WHERE DID THE GOSPELS COME FROM?

The Bible is an amazing source of what some early Christians thought and taught. In the case of the apostle Paul, we have letters actually written by him almost 2000 years ago! In the case of Jesus, we have nothing written by him, but we have four accounts of his life and teachings, which are the four Gospels of the New Testament. Two of these, Matthew and Luke, apparently used Mark as a source, because for some passages all three have the same text with only minor changes.[11] This means that what these three "synoptic" Gospels have in common, including the timeline, is only one version retold and not three independent sources as would be preferable for corroboration of the stories.

Matthew and Luke revised the Gospel of Mark and added additional material, some of which is unique to each of them. This explains the substantial differences at the beginning and the end of the story. The Gospel of Mark had no story of the birth of Jesus, but Matthew and Luke added different versions that did not agree, and each added a different version of the resurrection of Jesus to the brief account in Mark. Matthew and Luke also apparently shared another source in common (called "Q" by scholars).[12] This common source, comprised of the overlap of Matthew and Luke but not Mark, includes some of the most famous teachings of Jesus such as the Golden Rule ("do to others as you would have them do to you") and the

---

9. Levine, *Misunderstood Jew*, 78–86.

10. H. W. Basser, "Gospel and Talmud," ch. 17 in Levine et al., *Historical Jesus*.

11. This relationship between the synoptic Gospels is widely accepted, see for example Ehrman, *New Testament*; Harris, *New Testament*; Levine et al., *Historical Jesus*, 1–39.

12. This hypothetical source is called "Q" after the German "Quelle" or "source"; Ehrman, *New Testament*, ch. 6; Koester, *Ancient Christian Gospels*, 128–71.

command to "love your enemies." This additional common source provides information about Jesus that did not come from Mark. The Gospel of John does not clearly share sources in common with the other three, containing different and possibly independent versions of some things and much that is not in the other Gospels.

As discussed previously (chapter 2), at least some of the details in the stories of Jesus are not literally true, and this is clear because the different versions are contradictory. Furthermore, we do not have Jesus' teachings in his own words because he spoke Aramaic, the common language of Jews in Palestine, while the Gospels were written in Greek. His words as we have them were translated into Greek by his followers, with only a few Aramaic words remaining (Mark 5:41, 15:34). There are versions of the four Gospels in ancient Syriac, similar to Aramaic, but they were translated into Syriac from the Greek versions so they still do not preserve the original words of Jesus.[13] We just do not have them. This is the bad news, but the good news is that we have more information about Jesus than for almost anyone else from ancient times, especially anyone poor! The fact that some of the same things are reported by multiple sources provides some confirmation that in fact they actually happened. This is about as good as it gets in the study of ancient history.

Just going by the books themselves and the earliest traditions about them, it is likely that the four Gospels were written by the followers of Jesus' followers (or the followers of the followers of his followers), in the second half of the first century CE. The writers seem to have been aware of the disastrous Jewish War with the Romans that happened in 70 CE (see Mark 13:14, Luke 21:20), so these books may have been written soon after that, several decades after Jesus, perhaps in response to the fact that most of the original disciples of Jesus had died by that time. The author of the Gospel of Luke, who probably also wrote the Acts of the Apostles, told us what he intended in the opening of the book:

> Inasmuch as many have undertaken to compile a narrative of the things which have been accomplished among us, just as they were delivered to us by those who from the beginning were eyewitness-es and ministers of the word, it seemed good to me also, having followed all things closely for some time past, to write an orderly account for you, most excellent Theophilus [literally, "Friend of

---

13. Koester, *Ancient Christian Gospels*, 403–11; Caruso, *Problems With Peshitta Primacy*; Gurtner, *The Gospel of Mark in Syriac Christianity*.

God"], that you may know the truth concerning the things of which you have been informed. (Luke 1:1–4, RSV)

Luke, as I call the unknown author, intended to give the facts as he understood them, drawing from various sources. He did not intend his Gospel to be an allegory or fiction. He told us plainly he was not an eyewitness, but he collected what information he could and put it together in "an orderly account." The historical accuracy of his account is dependent on the reliability of his sources and his care in compiling them. Looking at what he wrote, his sources included the Gospel of Mark, plus additional sources shared with Matthew ("Q"), and some information not found in the other Gospels. Tradition has it that the author of the Gospel of Luke was a companion of the apostle Paul (Luke "the beloved physician" mentioned in Colossians 4:14), based on the fact that the Acts of the Apostles has some narrative written in the first person perspective, but there is no further evidence about who he was or where he got his information. Although he intended to write a factual account, like anyone he could have made mistakes writing decades after the events with few written records,[14] and he had his own bias as a Christian believer and follower of Paul.

The authors of the Gospel of John (they referred to themselves as plural) told us they got their information from one of Jesus' own disciples (John 21:24). In fact, they said he was the most special "beloved disciple," present at the Last Supper and the crucifixion of Jesus, but this person was never named, and may not have been one of the twelve "chosen" disciples. It is a mystery why he was not named, and there are few clues as to his identity.[15] The beloved disciple traditionally has been identified as the disciple John the son of Zebedee, one of the inner-circle of the chosen twelve. This tradition arose in the second century as Christians attempted to connect the book to a prominent disciple. Even if the beloved disciple was named John, a common name, there is no evidence that he actually was John the son of Zebedee.

---

14. It appears that Luke made a factual error when he said Jesus was born during the reign of Herod the Great ("King of Judea," Luke 1:5), when Quirinius was governor of Syria (Luke 2:2–3). According to other Roman and Jewish sources, Quirinius was governor of Syria (and had a census) but not until ten years after the death of King Herod. See Ehrman, *New Testament*, p. 18; Levine and Brettler, *Jewish Annotated New Testament*, p. 101; Josephus, *Antiquities*, 17.354, 18.1–2, *War*, 2.117, 7.253.

15. Lazarus (John 11), and James the brother of Jesus have been suggested as candidates for the beloved disciple.

Regardless of who "the beloved disciple" was, the connection with this disciple raises the possibility that the Gospel of John contains firsthand eyewitness accounts. As with Luke, it is impossible to know how direct the connection really was between the authors of the final version and their sources. John is much different from the other versions of the life of Jesus, and seems to reflect a time late in the first century CE when Christian Jews were being excluded from Jewish synagogues (John 9:22), so most historians date it later than the other Gospels. John also shows a trend toward emphasizing the deity of Christ over his humanity, another suggestion of a later date. This can be seen, for example, by comparing the accounts of the arrest and crucifixion of Jesus from Mark and John. Finally, a late date is suggested by the fact that John replaced much of the future expectation of the Kingdom of God with an emphasis on a spiritual life in the present. Still, in cases where John does not agree with the other Gospels it is possible that John is correct, as discussed previously in connection with the day of Jesus' arrest and execution (chapter 2).

After these books were written, they were copied for hundreds of years before our earliest surviving copies were made, with variations creeping in along the way, sometimes large, sometimes small.[16] For example, the earliest available texts of the Gospel of Mark end with Mark 16:8—the women go to the tomb of Jesus, see an angel who tells them Jesus is risen, and then flee in astonishment and tell no one.[17] It is possible the original ending was lost, but this short ending is consistent with the rest of Mark where no one, not even his closest followers, ever really understands what Jesus is up to. The short ending also explains why the authors of Matthew and Luke found it necessary to independently expand their accounts of the resurrection, using different sources. Later scribes attempted to "correct" this abrupt ending of Mark by adding additional verses (Mark 16:9–20), sometimes with other variations. This second, later ending appears to depend on the resurrection accounts in Luke and John, summarizing some of the main events.

The earliest known tradition about the authorship of the Gospel of Mark said that Mark was an interpreter for the apostle Peter when this prominent disciple of Jesus was in Rome, and that Mark gathered his material from Peter's sermons. Mark himself did not know Jesus and lacked a systematic arrangement of his sayings and actions, putting them together in a story as best he could. This tradition was quoted by the fourth-century

---

16. Koester, *Ancient Christian Gospels*; Ehrman, *Orthodox Corruption of Scripture*.

17. For discussion see Ehrman, *Misquoting Jesus*, 65–69.

Christian historian Eusebius, as written by the second-century church leader Papias.[18] It could simply be a guess or an attempt to give Mark an apostolic connection, but even this oldest tradition did not claim that Mark was an eyewitness or had complete information. Taken on its own terms, the Gospel of Mark seems unlikely to be based on Peter as a source, given its original lack of an account of Peter and the disciples seeing the risen Jesus; still, it is an intriguing possibility. Papias also had a tradition about the authorship of the Gospel of Matthew, that it was written in Hebrew by the disciple Levi (Matt. 9:9, Mark 2:14), but our Gospel of Matthew does not match his description. Our Matthew was written in Greek using the Greek translation of the Jewish scriptures, and incorporated Mark that was in Greek. We do not really know where these books came from except that Christians were reading them by the second century CE and wondering who wrote them, and arguing about which ones were authentic.

---

18. Eusebius, *Historia Ecclesiastica*, 3.39.15; Harris, *New Testament*, 103, 130.

4

The Message of Jesus the Christ

THE KINGDOM OF HEAVEN IS AT HAND

The writers of the New Testament were trying to persuade readers that Jesus is the Christ, the Savior foretold by the prophets. The Gospel of John explicitly states that "these things were written that you may believe that Jesus is the Christ, the Son of God, and that believing you may have life in his name" (John 20:31). Taking the writings of the New Testament as a whole, two things are clear: the people who wrote them believed that Jesus was the Jewish Messiah, the Christ, and they believed the end of the world as they knew it was just around the corner, it was "at hand" (Matt. 3:17, Mark 1:15, Rom. 13:11, 1 Cor. 7:29, 10:11, 1 Peter 4:7). This would result in a climactic triumph of good over evil, as in the familiar Lord's prayer: "Your kingdom come, your will be done on earth as it is in heaven" (Matt. 6:10). This was an apocalyptic way of thinking, and it was common among Jews at the time of Jesus, a version of the expectation of the Messiah who would usher in an age of peace.

The synoptic Gospels tell us that Jesus said this would happen soon. The urgent expectation is toned-down in John but still a strong undercurrent (John 1:45, 5:25–29, 6:40, 11:23–27, 21:20–24). In Matthew (24), Mark (13) and Luke (17, 21), Jesus describes the incredible things that will happen leading up to the Kingdom of Heaven on earth. He tells his disciples to be watching and ready, that "this generation will not pass away before all these things take place." He describes how the "Son of Man" will come in power with his holy angels, saying, "Truly I say to you, there are some standing here who will not taste death before they see that the Kingdom of God has come with power" (Mark 8:38—9:1, Matt. 16:28). In this kingdom, his twelve chosen disciples will sit on twelve thrones next to him, as judges for the restored twelve tribes of Israel (Matt. 19:28, Luke 22:30, Mark 10:35–37).[1] Jesus tells his disciples to spread the news, and that they "will not have gone through all the towns of Israel" before the end comes (Matt. 10:24). His message is simple: "Repent, for the Kingdom of Heaven is at hand" (Matt. 4:17).

The word translated "repent" in this message of Jesus is the verb form of the Greek *metanoia*, meaning to have a change of mind. Perhaps the apostle Paul was thinking of this when he wrote, "Be not conformed to this world, but be transformed by the renewing of your mind" (Rom. 12:2). This transformation occurs in the individual in the present, and also prepares the believer for the coming Kingdom of Heaven. Like Jesus in the Gospels, Paul told his followers to be ready for the end to come very soon (Rom. 13:11). He argued that there was not much point in getting married and raising a family, because "the time is short" (1 Cor. 7:29). His converts in Thessalonica apparently expected they would all live to see the coming Kingdom of God. Because of this, Paul wrote to reassure them that believers who had died would be resurrected into the new life along with the living, and all would be changed "in the twinkling of an eye" (1 Thess. 4:13–18). He seems to have expected that he and most of them would be alive when this happened, given that he wrote: "we who are alive and remain until the coming of the Lord" will be caught up to meet him in the air.

The apocalyptic, messianic message of the first Christians is not surprising, given the Jewish culture of the time.[2] The Dead Sea Scrolls, for example, reveal a Jewish religious community at the time of Jesus that was steeped in apocalyptic expectation.[3] In the Gospels, Jesus and most of his opponents agreed on the basic messianic idea, they just disagreed about the immediacy of it and the role of Jesus in it (John 7:40–52, for example). The apostle Paul was a member of an influential Jewish sect called the Pharisees, before he had his conversion experience and began preaching that Jesus was the Messiah (Philip. 3:5). As a Pharisee, he already had much in common with the original followers of Jesus, including an apocalyptic expectation and a belief in the resurrection of the dead, which would occur

---

1. See discussion by Ehrman, *Jesus: Apocalyptic Prophet*, 186.

2. Levine, *Misunderstood Jew*, ch. 2; Newsome, *Greeks, Romans, Jews*, 240–47.

3. P. Flint, "Jesus and the Dead Sea Scrolls," 110–31 in Levine et al., *Historical Jesus*; Schiffman, *Reclaiming the Dead Sea Scrolls*, ch. 20, 21.

with the coming of the Messiah (Matt. 12:23–28, 16:1; Acts 15:5, 23:6–9; 1 Thess. 4:13–17). His acceptance of Jesus meant to him that the end he already expected would be coming very soon, under the lordship of Jesus the Messiah ("the Lord Jesus Christ").

The Jewish historian Flavius Josephus (born 37 CE) lived in Galilee (where Jesus also was from) in the decades after Jesus. He later wrote an account of the conflicts between Jews and Romans that resulted in the destruction of Jerusalem in 70 CE. He described several instances of prophets who stirred up crowds with pronouncements that God would soon restore the nation of Israel. This apocalyptic fervor challenged Roman authority, so the Romans had little tolerance for it. Two would-be prophets, called Theudas and "the Egyptian," were mentioned by Josephus and also in the New Testament (Acts 5:36, 21:38). In both cases, they raised a group of followers and were killed by the Romans.[4]

LOVE YOUR NEIGHBOR AS YOURSELF

Jesus was not attempting a military overthrow of Roman rule, but rather expected that this would happen soon through divine intervention. His message went beyond the mere restoration of Jewish freedom, and was based on mercy, compassion, communal sharing, and forgiveness for all. By doing these things we will show ourselves to be the children of our Father in heaven (Matt. 5:44–45). We will be doing God's will "on earth as it is in heaven" (Matt. 6:10). Jesus preached a personal transformation that happens in the present, and taught people to think of God as their loving father who would provide for them:

> [Jesus said] Therefore I tell you, do not be anxious about your life, what you shall eat, nor about your body, what you shall put on. For life is more than food, and the body more than clothing. Consider the ravens: they neither sow nor reap, they have neither storehouse nor barn, and yet God feeds them. Of how much more value are you than the birds! And which of you by being anxious can add a cubit to his span of life? If then you are not able to do as small a thing as that, why are you anxious about the rest? Consider the lilies, how they grow; they neither toil nor spin; yet I tell you, even Solomon in all his glory was not arrayed like one of these. But if God so clothes the grass which is alive in the field today and

---

4. Ehrman, *Jesus: Apocalyptic Prophet*, 117, 158; C. Evans, "Josephus on John the Baptist and other Jewish prophets," ch. 2 in Levine et al., *Historical Jesus*.

tomorrow is thrown into the oven, how much more will he clothe you, O men of little faith!

And do not seek what you are to eat and what you are to drink, nor be of anxious mind. For all the nations of the world seek these things; and your Father knows that you need them. Instead, seek his kingdom, and these things shall be yours as well. Fear not, little flock, for it is your Father's good pleasure to give you the kingdom. Sell your possessions, and give alms [to the poor]; provide yourselves with purses that do not grow old, with a treasure in the heavens that does not fail, where no thief approaches and no moth destroys. For where your treasure is, there will your heart be also. (Luke 12:22–34, RSV)

Jesus called for complete trust in a loving God, here and now. Consistent with this, he was known as a great healer and exorcist, but often told people it was their own faith that healed them (Mark 5:34, 10:52, 7:50). He said that God is the friend of the poor, downtrodden, and oppressed, and these will be honored in the Kingdom of Heaven rather than the rich, powerful, or self-righteous. "Blessed are you poor, for yours is the Kingdom of Heaven," but "woe to the rich" (Luke 10:20–24). The way to be great in God's kingdom is to humble yourself as the servant of others (Mark 9:35), and "it is more blessed to give than to receive" (Acts 20:35). Jesus also may have been more open to women and non-Jews than many of his contemporaries (Luke 7:2–10, 10:39, John 4), though he probably saw his mission as being primarily to and about the Jews (Matt. 10:5–6, 15:24, Mark 7:25–30, Acts 10:28, 11:18).

The emphasis that Jesus placed on compassion was different from some other prophets described by Josephus, but it was not unique.[5] As a Jewish prophet and teacher, Jesus based his message on the Jewish scriptures and traditions surrounding them. Some Old Testament prophets had said that God wanted mercy and justice more than sacrifices and rituals (Mic. 6:8, Hos. 6:6). Jesus was quoting Leviticus (19:18) in the Torah, the Law of Moses, when he said "Love your neighbor as yourself" (Mark 12:31). One of the most famous teachings of Jesus is known as the Golden Rule, "Do to others as you would have them do to you." A version of the Golden Rule was already known in Jesus' time, from the Jewish book of Tobit, probably written two to three centuries before Jesus, copies of which were found among the Dead Sea Scrolls.[6] The renowned rabbi Hillel, who died while Jesus was a young boy, was quoted saying, "That which is hateful

---

5. Levine, *Misunderstood Jew*, ch. 1, 6.

6. Tobit 4:15; VanderKam, *An Introduction to Early Judaism*, 69–71.

to you, do not do to your fellow. That is the whole Law [of Moses]; the rest is explanation."[7] Jesus may have been expressing agreement with Hillel when he said something very similar about the Golden Rule as the fulfillment of "the Law and the prophets" (Matt. 7:12). John the Baptist also was a contemporary and associate of Jesus, and like Jesus combined a message of righteousness and repentance with an apocalyptic urgency (Matt. 3:2, 17; Luke 3:2–18). The connections with Tobit, Hillel, and John the Baptist, and the constant references by Jesus in the Gospels to the Jewish scriptures, confirm that Jesus was speaking within a tradition familiar to his hearers.[8]

Jesus had a radical interpretation of some of the commandments, but even this was consistent with a tradition of rabbis expounding deeper meanings in the commandments. The famous Sermon on the Mount in the Gospel of Matthew contains numerous examples where Jesus extended a commandment to include not only actions but also intent (Matt. 5–7). "Blessed are the pure in heart, for they are the ones who will see God," he said. It is not enough to refrain from murder; hatred is also a violation of the commandment "Do not kill." Likewise, if a man lusts after a woman who is not his wife, he has committed adultery in his heart. If you have offended someone, be reconciled to your brother before offering your sacrifices to God; the reconciliation is what God really wants. In these examples Jesus focused on the heart as the source of righteousness.

Concerning the commandment to "love your neighbor as yourself," in the parable of the good Samaritan, Jesus extended the definition of "neighbor" to include anyone who needed help (Luke 10:25–37). He also made it a question not of "who is my neighbor?" or "who am I obligated to consider?"; but rather, "am I being a neighbor to those in need?" In this parable, a man left for dead by robbers was ignored by priests who did not want the trouble of helping him, but he was helped by a Samaritan who went to great effort and personal expense to care for the man. The Jewish audience of Jesus would have caught the irony of this story, where the hero was a Samaritan, an outsider whom many Jews believed to be impure and rejected by God, while the priests passed by and looked the other way, missing the true meaning of the commandments they claimed to serve.[9] The admoni-

---

7. Talmud, *Shabbat* 31a; Newsome, *Greeks, Romans, Jews*, 317–18.

8. H.W. Basser, "Gospel and Talmud," ch. 17 in Levine et al., *Historical Jesus*; Levine, *Misunderstood Jew*.

9. For discussion see Harris, *New Testament*, 66–67, 173–74; Levine, *Misunderstood Jew*, 144–49.

tion to treat everyone as a neighbor is consistent with the radical meaning Jesus gave to other commandments, summed up in his admonition to love not only your neighbors, but also your enemies:

> Love your enemies, do good to those who hate you, bless those who curse you, pray for those who abuse you. To him who strikes you on the cheek, offer the other also; and from him who takes away your coat do not withhold even your shirt. Give to every one who begs from you; and of him who takes away your goods do not ask them again. *And as you wish that men would do to you, do so to them.*
> ... love your enemies, and do good, and lend, expecting nothing in return; and your reward will be great, and you will be sons of the Most High; for he is kind to the ungrateful and the selfish. (Luke 6:27–35, RSV, emphasis added)

> You have heard that it was said, "You shall love your neighbor and hate your enemy," but I say to you, Love your enemies ... (Matt. 5:43–44, RSV)

Love your enemies? This is a shocking statement, in any culture! The Golden Rule as taught by Jesus in this passage also emphasizes active good rather than simply refraining from harm. This message is consistent with the parable of the good Samaritan, where it is the action of helping the injured man that is commended.

These sayings of Jesus about the central importance of love show up in paraphrased form in the letters of Paul, who may have heard them from other Christians. Paul, like Jesus, said all the commandments are summed up in the commandment to "love your neighbor as yourself," and added, "Love does no wrong to a neighbor, therefore love is the fulfillment of the law" (Rom. 13:9–10, Gal. 5:14). Paul did not say "love your enemies" in his known letters, but he wrote things very similar, which could be direct quotes from Jesus or a restatement of his teachings:

> Bless those who persecute you; bless and do not curse them. Rejoice with those who rejoice, weep with those who weep. Live in harmony with one another; do not be haughty, but associate with the lowly; never be conceited. Repay no one evil for evil, but take thought for what is noble in the sight of all. If possible, so far as it depends upon you, live peaceably with all.
> Beloved, never avenge yourselves, but leave it to the wrath of God; for it is written, "Vengeance is mine, I will repay, says the Lord." No, "if your enemy is hungry, feed him; if he is thirsty, give

him drink; for by so doing you will heap burning coals [of shame] upon his head."

Do not be overcome by evil, but overcome evil with good. (Rom. 12:14–21, RSV)

The sentence about "if your enemy is hungry feed him . . . " in this passage is a direct quote from the Old Testament book of Proverbs (25:21–22), demonstrating that even these radical ethical teachings were rooted in an understanding of the Jewish scriptures. These and similar statements by Paul, written perhaps two to three decades before the synoptic Gospels, comprise the earliest known written record of these principles as part of the Christian tradition.

Consistent with the admonition to "love your enemies," Jesus had some radical teachings about forgiveness. According to the Gospels, he told people their sins were forgiven, something his opponents saw as presumptuous because only God can forgive sins (Mark 2:7). Jesus said that God wants to forgive us, we need only repent, a message illustrated by the parable of the lost son (Luke 15:11–32). The son took his inheritance from his father and wasted it, then returned wishing only to live as one of his father's servants. His father saw him coming and ran to him, telling him all was forgiven. Jesus told his disciples to forgive without limit (Matt. 18:22). Perhaps most significant, Jesus said God will forgive our sins, if we will forgive those who sin against us: "Forgive and you will be forgiven" (Matt. 6:15, Luke 6:37). Jesus lived up to this teaching when on the cross he prayed, "Father forgive them, for they do not know what they are doing" (Luke 23:24).

The teaching of forgiveness was at the heart of the message of Jesus in the Gospels. Much of the discussion with his opponents centered on the question of how a person can be right with God. Jesus said all that is required is a repentant heart and the willingness to forgive others, as illustrated by the parable of the Pharisee and the tax collector. Tax collectors were despised as Roman collaborators who enriched themselves at the expense of others:

> Two men went up into the temple to pray, one a Pharisee and the other a tax collector. The Pharisee stood and prayed thus with himself, "God, I thank thee that I am not like other men, extortioners, unjust, adulterers, or even like this tax collector. I fast twice a week, I give tithes of all that I get."
>
> But the tax collector, standing far off, would not even lift up his eyes to heaven, but beat his breast, saying, "God, be merciful to me a sinner!"

> I tell you, this man went down to his house justified rather
> than the other; for every one who exalts himself will be humbled,
> but he who humbles himself will be exalted. (Luke 8:10–14, RSV)

Like some of the other parables of Jesus, this story conveyed a surprising message. God was willing to forgive the despised tax-collector who recognized his sin and asked for mercy, but not the self-righteous Pharisee who lacked humility. God forgave the one who thought he did not deserve it.

This discussion of the teachings and message of Jesus has been drawn mainly from the synoptic Gospels. Jesus in these Gospels teaches in parables and wise sayings, and expounds the meaning of the scriptures, a portrait consistent with stories about prophets and teachers preserved in later Jewish traditions. The Gospel of Mark declares that he did not say anything publicly without using a parable (Mark 4:34). Jesus in the Gospel of John has a very different style, speaking in long philosophical discourses and hardly ever using a parable. The emphasis in John is on the believer's relationship in this life with the Holy Spirit, the Comforter. Those who believe in Jesus are "born of the spirit" and will have eternal life (John 3). Most historians conclude that the synoptic Gospels are probably closer to the actual words of Jesus than the Gospel of John. Still, the basic themes of John and the other three Gospels are similar: Jesus is the Messiah and Savior; his kingdom is soon to come or is already arriving; and righteousness consists in loving, forgiving, and serving one another. In John, Jesus tells his disciples, "a new commandment I give to you, that you love one another as I have loved you. . . . By this all men will know that you are my disciples" (John 13:34); and, "This is my commandment that you love one another" (John 15:12). These perhaps are references to the commandments of Moses, similar to the idea that the Law and the prophets are fulfilled in loving one another. Although the Jesus of John seems almost too exalted to be human, he washes the disciples' feet on the night before his death, to demonstrate his message of love (John 13). The Gospel of John more generally is about Jesus as the light of the world and giver of life, rather than the coming Kingdom of God. There is still the idea that Christ will return, but this is less important than the fact that he is with us through the Holy Spirit or Comforter he has sent (John 16, 17).

Also found in John is a dramatic story of Jesus facing down the accusers of a woman caught in adultery, and telling her after they have left, "Neither do I condemn you; go, and sin no more" (John 8:3–11). This story, popular in movie dramatizations, shows characteristics of Jesus familiar from the synoptic Gospels. Jesus had compassion for the oppressed (a woman threatened with stoning), and was merciful and forgiving. Jesus advocated righteousness, but opposed self-righteousness and condemnation of others, and he demanded that those accusing the woman look first at themselves. He was accused of laxness concerning the Jewish laws, but defeated his opponents by shaming or confounding them: "Let him who is without sin among you be the first to cast a stone at her." This story could fit in one of the other Gospels, and in fact it was found in some early versions of Luke, and was not present in some early manuscripts of John. It may be that this story of the woman caught in adultery was transmitted independently, and eventually was preserved by inclusion in the Gospel of John.[10]

Important elements of the message of Jesus are summarized in what is probably his most familiar saying, known as the Lord's Prayer, taught by Jesus to his disciples and recited today by millions around the world. This prayer contains the elements of reliance on God as a loving father, the hope of the coming Kingdom of Heaven on earth, and forgiveness of others as the key to being right before God. This principle of forgiveness is spelled out in a comment following the prayer in the Gospel of Matthew:

> [Jesus said] Pray then like this: Our Father who is in heaven, holy is your name. Your kingdom come, your will be done, on earth as it is in heaven. Give us this day our daily bread; and forgive us our debts [sins], as we also have forgiven our debtors; And lead us not into temptation, but deliver us from evil.
>
> *For if you forgive men their trespasses, your heavenly Father also will forgive you*; but if you do not forgive men their trespasses, neither will your Father forgive your trespasses. (Matt. 6:9–15, emphasis added)

The Jewish scriptures, and Jewish teachers and prophets such as Hillel and John the Baptist, were part of the background from which Jesus emerged and in which he lived. The Gospel writers were careful to say that Jesus was greater than John the Baptist, but it seems clear that John was a mentor and associate of Jesus, and Jesus was baptized by John as John baptized his other disciples (Mark 1, Luke 3, John 1, 3). Consistent with this, the message of Jesus was similar to that of John the Baptist, who proclaimed the imminent arrival of the Messiah and the judgment of God, combined with strong ethical teachings (Matt. 3). What was most unusual about Jesus was that his followers said he actually was the Messiah and they

---

10. Ehrman, *Misquoting Jesus*, 63–65; Harris, *New Testament*, 202–203.

proclaimed this even after he was crucified. Jesus' disciples Peter and John, and his brother James (one of four brothers of Jesus[11] named in Mark 6:3) led these Jewish Christians based in Jerusalem, who spread the message of Jesus the Christ and the Kingdom of Heaven (Acts 21:17–22, Gal. 1:18–19).

FROM CHRIST TO CHRISTIANITY

The followers of Jesus grew old and died, yet the world remained little changed and the Kingdom of God did not come in power on earth as they had predicted. A poignant example of this disappointment is found in the closing chapter of the Gospel of John. The book seems to end in chapter 20, but then continues with a story about the risen Jesus, Peter, and the un-named "beloved disciple." The Christians who produced the Gospel of John believed that Jesus had said their beloved disciple would see the return of Jesus in his lifetime (John 21:20–23). They found it necessary to explain that Jesus must not have said this exactly, they must have misunderstood. Reading between the lines: the beloved disciple, a follower of Jesus who led this Christian group, had died, dashing their hopes that Christ would return in his lifetime. The Gospel of John, with its reduced emphasis on the future apocalypse, reflects the transition of Christianity away from hope in the future to an emphasis on experiencing "eternal life" in the present through the Holy Spirit, the Comforter (John 5:24, 14:16–21). The closing chapter of John reveals that even among this community the apocalyptic expectation was very strong.

If this is true, why have so many Christians down through history, including me, not noticed that the New Testament was wrong about the imminent end of the world? The answer is simple: we assumed that the Bible could not be wrong, and adopted other explanations. The traditional alternative explanations are: (1) Jesus did not mean it was going to happen right away, this interpretation must be a mistake, and (2) God's ways are not our ways; we just do not understand. Over time, the urgent hope of the coming Kingdom of Heaven became more distant, and Christians replaced the initial focus on the end of the world with a focus on individual life and death. Everyone is going to die at the end of a short life "and after that the judgment" (Heb. 9:27), so this is enough to retain the urgency of the New Testament, as seen in modern "fire and brimstone" preaching. It is apparent from an unbiased reading that most of the time this was not what Jesus in

---

11. For discussion of Jesus' brothers see Harris, *New Testament*, 248.

the synoptic Gospels or Paul in his letters were talking about when they spoke of salvation. They were promising a dramatic transformation of the world that was to happen in that generation.

Jesus was quoted as saying that nobody, including himself, knows the day or hour when the end will happen and the Kingdom of God will come in power (Mark 13:32; see chapter 6). Christians have emphasized this to show that he did not really mean it was "at hand." The Second Epistle of Peter contains a response to "scoffers" who pointed out that the end had not come as Christians had predicted. We are told to be steadfast in belief, and that "God is not slack concerning his promise," because "a thousand years is as one day" to God, and God has his own reasons, giving more time for people to be saved (2 Pet. 3:1–13). The book of Hebrews shows the same concern, saying we must be patient to receive the promise of his coming, that he will come and "will not tarry" (Heb. 10:36–37). Apparently, people were concerned that he was tarrying so it was necessary to say something about it. Some Christians went so far as to say that the Day of the Lord had already happened. Paul's second letter to the Thessalonians was written in response to this claim, to reassure them that some things had to happen first (2 Thess. 2:1–12). The Second Epistle to Timothy also warns against teachers who claimed that "the resurrection" had already happened (2 Tim. 2:18). Other Christians, represented by writings outside the New Testament such as the Gospel of Thomas, rejected the idea of a future Kingdom of God.[12] The Epistle of James, in response to these concerns, tells us to "Be patient . . . until the coming of the Lord . . . be patient, establish your hearts, for the coming of the Lord is at hand" (Jas. 5:7–8). This is where Christianity has remained for nearly 2000 years, hovering between urgent expectation of the Second Coming of Christ as the New Testament proclaims, and the need to be patient and continue with ordinary human lives.

WAS JESUS WRONG ABOUT THE END OF THE WORLD?

As a person who believed in traditional Christianity, one of the most challenging conclusions to come from an honest study of the Bible was the fact that the first Christians were wrong about the immediacy of God's kingdom on earth. It is clear beyond reasonable doubt that the people who wrote the New Testament believed this would happen soon, and they believed this was what Jesus proclaimed. Why are we to repent? Because the time is fulfilled

---

12. Pagels, *Beyond Belief*, ch. 2.

and the Kingdom of God is at hand. From what do we need to be saved? The coming destruction and judgment. When is this going to happen? While some of the people hearing this are still alive, in the generation of Jesus and his disciples. It is no wonder that many Christians today who read the New Testament believe the end is coming soon, because that is what it says! This is an attractive and powerful message, that all the suffering and evil in the world will soon come to a miraculous end, consistent with the plan of a loving God.

A common explanation used to resolve this issue is that Jesus could not have been referring to his own generation; instead he must have meant the generation who saw the signs he predicted. This is the basis of the bestselling book by Hal Lindsey called *The Late Great Planet Earth*,[13] the more recent *Left Behind* series,[14] and the whole vast industry of books and preachers interpreting the signs of the times.[15] Lindsey said the formation of the nation of Israel in the late 1940s was a sign of the end, so everything would wrap up within a generation of that time. As I studied the Bible, I realized that Paul and the other New Testament authors believed that Jesus was talking about them, not providing clues for believers 2000 years later. Even if Jesus really meant it might be 2000 years, this was not what the New Testament authors told us. They said some things had to happen first, but it would all happen soon in their time.

The urgent apocalyptic message of the New Testament is challenging to Christians because it demonstrates two things:

1. The New Testament authors believed the end would come in their time, and they were wrong about this.

2. If the New Testament is correct in its portrayal of Jesus, then Jesus was wrong about the immediacy of God's kingdom on earth. If not, then the New Testament is wrong about Jesus and his message.

Can this really be true? Did Jesus teach the imminent end of the age in his own time? It is clear that this is what the New Testament says. There are some things in dispute in the academic world of Biblical studies, but this is not one of them. There is broad agreement that the New Testament is urgently apocalyptic and portrays Jesus this way, as anyone can see who reads it with an open mind. The writings reveal a growing concern and confusion

---

13. Lindsey and Carlson, *Late Great Planet Earth*.

14. LaHaye and Jenkins, *Left Behind*.

15. For further discussion see Ehrman, *Jesus: Apocalyptic Prophet*, ch. 1; Ehrman, *Misquoting Jesus*, 1–16.

over this as time wore on and the end did not happen (John 21:20–24; 2 Thess. 2; 2 Pet. 3; Heb. 10:36–37).

I first encountered the idea that Jesus was wrong about the end of the world when I was a teenager reading the Christian author C.S. Lewis. In an essay called *The World's Last Night*,[16] Lewis made the point that Jesus was human (as Christians profess to believe), and a person cannot be fully human if he knows everything, because uncertainty is part of being human. The Gospels also say Jesus slept, and if he really slept like a human he was unconscious and unaware of his surroundings (as Mark 4:38 implies), not completely aware and omniscient. Likewise, Lewis said, Jesus' mistake about the timing of God's kingdom was just another example that he was human, and did not know for sure when it would happen, as he is quoted as saying (Mark 13:32). As a young Christian, I liked this interpretation because Lewis accepted the Bible at its literal word that Jesus taught the end would come soon. I could see this and was uncomfortable with attempts to explain it away. Lewis also saw no need to reject Christian faith on this basis. This helped me begin to take the Bible at its word, and to understand what the New Testament was really about.

There is a broad consensus among scholars and historians that Jesus in the New Testament proclaimed an imminent apocalypse, but this consensus does not include the many churches, publishers, Bible schools and even large universities that do not allow questioning of the Bible.[17] For example, Oral Roberts University supports a network of schools called the Oral Roberts University Educational Fellowship. Members of this network are expected to have curricula "built on the complete and uncompromised Word of God," and to support a Statement of Faith that begins: "We believe the Bible to be the inspired, authoritative, and infallible Word of God."[18] These statements reveal a commitment to a biased interpretation of the Bible, based on preconceptions about what it means and says. Both Jesus and the Bible are assumed to be the direct word of an omniscient God, so no human errors or inconsistencies are possible. Such prejudicial interpretation is incompatible with an honest assessment of the Bible as history. Outside of this fundamentalist religious sphere, there is wide agreement among Biblical scholars and historians that the Gospels portray Jesus as

---

16. Lewis, *World's Last Night*.

17. For a personal account of institutions with different Biblical perspectives, see Ehrman, *Misquoting Jesus*, 1–16.

18. Oral Roberts University, *Join ORUEF*.

urgently apocalyptic, as was John the Baptist, Paul, and virtually every other sympathetic voice in the New Testament—they believed the end was near. The truth of this is clear when the authors are allowed to speak in their own voices.

There are actually two questions involved in the prediction of an imminent end of the world as we know it. First, did Jesus and the Christian founders predict it would happen in their time? This question can be addressed historically, and the evidence is strong that they did predict this, as I have discussed. The second question is of a different kind: Were these predictions correct in their substance, even if the timing was not? Will our world end in a cataclysmic and mystical transformation to a new reality, the Kingdom of Heaven on earth, the triumph of good over evil? This is not a question that can be answered by evidence or a study of history. History can show what may have happened in the past, and by that can suggest what is likely to happen in the future, but the end of the world predicted by Christianity is a unique event that is not part of any pattern of history. History shows that it did not happen at the time of Jesus, or when Jerusalem was destroyed in 70 CE, or in the 2000 years since then, and this evidence suggests that it is unlikely to happen in the future; however, history cannot prove that such a miraculous transformation could never occur. This is a question of belief, not history.

THE KINGDOM OF GOD WITHIN YOU

Jesus of the New Testament was urgently apocalyptic, but a debate has arisen over the idea that the New Testament may have been wrong in this portrayal of Jesus.[19] Could it be that the ethical and mystical teachings of Jesus were the authentic part, and the apocalyptic part was added by over-zealous apocalyptic followers who misrepresented his true message? Proponents of this idea point to some of the parables of Jesus that describe the Kingdom of Heaven in mystical, non-apocalyptic terms, such as these from the Gospel of Matthew:

> The kingdom of heaven is like a grain of mustard seed which a man took and sowed in his field; it is the smallest of all seeds, but when it has grown it is the greatest of shrubs and becomes a tree, so that the birds of the air come and make nests in its branches.

---

19. Crossan, *Historical Jesus.*

> The kingdom of heaven is like leaven which a woman took
> and hid in three measures of flour, till it was all leavened.
>
> The kingdom of heaven is like treasure hidden in a field,
> which a man found and covered up; then in his joy he goes and
> sells all that he has and buys that field.
>
> Again, the kingdom of heaven is like a merchant in search of
> fine pearls, who, on finding one pearl of great value, went and sold
> all that he had and bought it. (Matt. 13:31–33, 44–46, RSV)

These parables seem to be about the spiritual reality of the Kingdom of Heaven in the present, not the apocalyptic Kingdom of Heaven coming soon with the Messiah. In the four Gospels, and apparently in the earliest sources, sayings such as these were intermixed with sayings of coming judgment, such as the parable of the net of fish:

> Again, the kingdom of heaven is like a net which was thrown into
> the sea and gathered fish of every kind; when it was full, men drew
> it ashore and sat down and sorted the good into vessels but threw
> away the bad. (Matt. 13:47–48, RSV)

This dual message of Christianity has sometimes been summarized by the phrase, "already—but not yet." The Kingdom of Heaven is already here in the person of Jesus and the Spirit of God in the world, but it is not yet fully realized "on earth as it is in heaven." Jesus in the Gospels had both sides to his message, but the mystical Jesus of here and now has often been more popular than the apocalyptic Jesus. In the 1990s this became a full-blown debate in the world of historical Jesus scholarship, as some people argued that Jesus was not really apocalyptic at all.

The Gospel of Thomas, a collection of sayings of Jesus discovered in Egypt in 1945, fueled this debate because it portrayed a Jesus who did not preach an apocalyptic message, and the origin appears to be relatively early (perhaps about 100 CE or even earlier). For example, in the Gospel of Luke, Jesus says we will not find the Kingdom of God by looking for it here or there, because "the Kingdom of God is within you" (Luke 17:20–21). Christians have often interpreted this as Jesus referring to himself "among you," but the Gospel of Thomas has two versions of this saying that make it explicitly clear that God's kingdom is already here, "spread out on the earth, but people do not see it" (Thomas 113), and "the kingdom is within you and without you" (Thomas 3). When asked when the new world would come, Jesus in Thomas responded, "What you look forward to is already here, but you do not recognize it" (Thomas 51). Thomas also has a different version of the parable of the net that is similar to other kingdom parables about finding something of great value:

> A man is like a wise fisher who cast his net into the sea, and drew it up full of fish. Among them he found a fine big fish. So he threw all the little fish back into the sea and without hesitation kept the big fish. (Thomas 8)[20]

The Jesus of Thomas was not an apocalyptic prophet; he was a mystic who uttered wise and cryptic sayings, guiding people to the truth within. This interpretation of Jesus generated a lot of excitement in academic circles,[21] and spilled over into some popular books.[22] This non-apocalyptic version of Jesus may be appealing, but requires asserting that the Bible was wrong about Jesus. For example, John D. Crossan, one of the leading proponents of this interpretation of Jesus, acknowledged that John the Baptist expected the Kingdom of Heaven soon on earth, and that Jesus agreed with him, but proposed that Jesus changed his mind after the death of John. Marcus Borg, in his popular book *Meeting Jesus Again for the First Time*, expressed this point of view as the basis for his understanding of Jesus:

> . . . what is being denied is the notion that Jesus expected the supernatural coming of the Kingdom of God as a world-ending event in his own generation. This growing scholarly consensus is a recent development. Over the last ten years, the image of Jesus as an eschatological [end-time] prophet, which dominated scholarship through the middle third of this century, has become very much a minority position.[23]

Borg portrayed Jesus as a healer, teacher, social prophet, and mystic, based on broad themes from the Gospels but without the messianic, apocalyptic message. He made important and valid points about Jesus as a mystic and social reformer, but his claim that the apocalyptic Jesus is a minority interpretation among historians was perhaps wishful thinking at the time, and is not true now two decades later. This debate shook up the academic consensus about the historical Jesus in a way that was probably healthy,

---

20. Various translations of the Gospel of Thomas are available, for example, Meyer, *Secret Teachings of Jesus*; Ehrman, *Lost Scriptures*. This quote is my own paraphrase.

21. Funk, et al., *Five Gospels*.

22. Borg, *Meeting Jesus Again*; Crossan, *Jesus, a Revolutionary Biography*; and other books by these authors.

23. Borg, *Meeting Jesus Again*, 29.

challenging assumptions and counterbalancing a one-sided emphasis on the apocalypse that sometimes missed other important facets of Jesus.[24]

The problem with this non-apocalyptic paradigm is that it requires throwing out most of the historical evidence for the life and teachings of Jesus and his associates! There is no good basis for rejecting the apocalyptic sayings but keeping others from the same sources, so this approach requires rejecting the New Testament in favor of hypothetical or fragmentary sources, and placing greater weight on the Gospel of Thomas.[25] The conjecture that Thomas represents an earlier and more authentic version of Christianity is interesting, but it is pure speculation and conflicts with evidence from the New Testament and the historical context of Jesus. With its non-apocalyptic, mystical version of Jesus, the Gospel of Thomas seems best understood as another example of how some Christians moved away from apocalyptic beliefs, to completely abandon the end-time perspective that had been an integral part of Christian beginnings.[26]

Some proponents of the non-apocalyptic Jesus have emphasized that Jesus was a person who believed he experienced God directly—what I have called a mystic—and this was the basis of much of his teaching. The Jewish scriptures are replete with examples of people who had visions and direct encounters with God, such as Moses, Samuel, Elijah and the other prophets of the Old Testament. Jesus and John the Baptist, as depicted in the Gospels, identified with this tradition of prophets who had a special connection with and message from God. Jesus and John were not simply teachers who interpreted the scriptures or the signs of the prophets, they believed that the Spirit of God was active in them speaking to the world. Certainly this was also true of the apostle Paul, who predicted an imminent apocalypse but placed the greatest emphasis on being filled with the Spirit of God in the present.[27] He said he was not taught this gospel by other people, but got it directly through revelation (Gal. 1:11). From the examples of Paul and John the Baptist, as well as Jesus, it is clear that mysticism in the present and belief in an apocalyptic future are not mutually exclusive.

---

24. For a balanced discussion see Levine et al., *Historical Jesus*, 1–39.

25. See Funk et al., *Five Gospels*; Crossan, *Historical Jesus*. For alternative points of view see Ehrman, *Jesus: Apocalyptic Prophet*, ch. 8; Johnson, *Real Jesus*.

26. Pagels, *Beyond Belief*; Ehrman, *Jesus: Apocalyptic Prophet*, ch. 13, 14.

27. See Johnson, *Real Jesus*, and other works by this author on the importance of mysticism in the beginnings of Christianity.

The Gospel of Luke quotes Jesus saying that God will freely give the Holy Spirit to all who ask (Luke 11:11–13). In the Gospel of John, Jesus says the Comforter, the Holy Spirit, will teach things beyond what Jesus told us, and will empower us to do even greater things than he did (John 14:12–26, 15:16–13). Many people in history and today have accepted this living Holy Spirit as a reality, believing in the active presence of God, a belief that is normal and encouraged in many churches. Having had mystical experiences myself in some small ways, I am inclined to think this was an important aspect of the historical Jesus, and one that has been under-appreciated by many historians. People really do have visions, revelations, and spiritual experiences, and this belief in the direct experience of God's spirit helps to explain much of what Jesus and his followers said and did.

SHARING EVERYTHING IN COMMON

Much of the teaching of Jesus was concerned with the present, living in the way of God even though God's kingdom has not yet fully come "on earth as it is in heaven." God's way requires empathy with the poor and oppressed. The gospel or "good news" message was "good news to the poor," but "woe to the rich" and to those who oppress or mistreat others (Luke 6:20–37). Jesus told his followers, "Sell your possessions, and give to the poor . . . for where your treasure is there will your heart be also" (Luke 12:33). According to the Acts of the Apostles, the first Christians in Jerusalem did exactly this—they sold their possessions and shared everything, under the leadership of the apostles:

> Now the company of those who believed were of one heart and soul, and no one said that any of the things which he possessed was his own, but they had everything in common. And with great power the apostles gave their testimony to the resurrection of the Lord Jesus, and great grace was upon them all. There was not a needy person among them, for as many as were possessors of lands or houses sold them, and brought the proceeds of what was sold and laid it at the apostles' feet; and distribution was made to each as any had need. (Acts 4:32–35, RSV)

In a society of great individual wealth such as the United States, sharing everything may not be received as "good news," but to people with nothing it may be very welcome. This way of life of the followers of Jesus may seem strange today, but there was a background and context in their world that made it easy to understand. The expectation of an imminent end may have encouraged the abandonment of worldly ties; however, the followers of Jesus were not the only ones nor were they the first Jews of their time to form a communal society as a way of life.

The people who produced the Dead Sea Scrolls had a communal settlement in the desert at a place called Qumran, on the shore of the Dead Sea, and they also had members who lived elsewhere in the region.[28] Josephus, the Jewish historian from Galilee, described a prominent sect called the Essenes that probably was connected with Qumran, and that provided a clear precedent for this way of life. They had similarities with Jesus and John the Baptist in doctrine as well as lifestyle. For example, it is likely the Essenes were expecting the Messiah (if the Dead Sea Scrolls are an indication), and they were critical of the Pharisees, as well as the Sadducees who ran the Jerusalem Temple.[29] Josephus, who claimed personal knowledge of the Essenes, described them as rejecting wealth and sharing everything in common:

> The Essenes . . . are despisers of riches, and so very communal as to earn our admiration. There is no one to be found among them who has more than another; for they have a law that those who come to join them must let whatever they have be common to the whole order, so that among them all there is no appearance of either poverty or excessive wealth. Everyone's possessions are intermingled with every other's possessions; as if they were all brothers with a single patrimony . . .
>
> They have no one city, but in every city dwell many of them; and if any of the sect arrive from elsewhere, all is made available to them as if it were their own; and they go to those they have never seen before as if long acquaintances. Thus they carry nothing at all with them in their journeys, except weapons for defense against thieves. Accordingly, in every city there is one appointed specifically to take care of strangers and to provide them with garments and other necessities . . .
>
> They change neither their garments nor their shoes until they are torn to pieces or worn out by time. They neither buy nor sell anything to one another, but each gives what he has to whomever needs it, and receives in exchange what he needs himself; and even

28. Newsome, *Greeks, Romans, Jews*, 149. Schiffman, *Reclaiming the Dead Sea Scrolls*, ch. 6; Schiffman. *Qumran and Jerusalem*, 147.

29. Josephus, *Antiquities* 18.1.5. For the works of Josephus see Goldberg, *Flavius Josephus Home Page*; Whiston, *Josephus*.

if there is nothing given any return, they are allowed to take anything they want from whomever they please.[30]

There are remarkable parallels between this description of the Essenes and the Christians in the book of Acts sharing all things in common. Also similar is the commission of Jesus to his disciples:

> Go your way; behold, I send you out as lambs in the midst of wolves. Carry no purse, no bag, no sandals; and salute no one on the road. Whatever house you enter, first say, Peace be to this house! And if a son of peace is there, your peace shall rest upon him; but if not, it shall return to you. And remain in the same house, eating and drinking what they provide, for the laborer deserves his wages; do not go from house to house. Whenever you enter a town and they receive you, eat what is set before you; heal the sick in it and say to them, The kingdom of God has come near to you." (Luke 10:3–9, RSV)

Similarly, when a rich young man asked Jesus how to "inherit eternal life," Jesus told him "you know the commandments," referring to the commandments of the Jewish Torah. When the man said he kept those commandments, Jesus told him, "You lack one thing; go, sell what you have, and give to the poor, and you will have treasure in heaven; and come, follow me." When the man left sorrowful, "for he had great possessions," Jesus remarked, "How hard it is for those who have riches to enter the Kingdom of Heaven!" (Mark 10:17–27). Identification with those who have nothing, and rejection of personal wealth, are recurrent themes in the Gospel stories of Jesus.

JESUS, PAUL AND THE ROLE OF WOMEN

The Essenes had other similarities with the followers of Jesus besides communal living and disdain of personal wealth, such as a rule against swearing an oath,[31] but there were clear differences. Like the Pharisees (as described by the Gospel writers and Josephus), the Essenes were strict about detailed observances of ritual laws such as refraining from work on the Sabbath,[32] whereas Jesus of the Gospels seems to have been more concerned with the

---

30. Josephus, *War* 2.8.2–4, Translation by Goldberg, "New Testament Parallels to the Works of Josephus," in *Flavius Josephus Home Page*.

31. Matt. 5:34–37; Josephus, *War* 2.8.6.

32. Josephus, *War* 2.8.9.

spirit of the laws rather than the letter (Matt. 12:1–14, for example). Another difference is that the Essenes as described by Josephus were all men; however, the group of Jesus and his disciples included some women (Matt. 27:55, Mark 15:40–42, Luke 8:1–3), and Jesus seems to have encouraged women to believe and participate in the hope of the Kingdom of God as much as men (Luke 10:38–42; John 4, 11:21–27, 20:1–20).

The Bible has its roots in ancient Judaism, a society where women were far from equal with men. According to Josephus, in Jewish courts only men were considered reliable witnesses.[33] Perhaps this was the reason Paul did not mention Mary Magdalene when he listed witnesses of the resurrection of Jesus (1 Cor. 15:5). Jewish writers from the time, such as Josephus[34] and the philosopher Philo of Alexandria,[35] expressed some disdain for women and esteemed the Essenes for separating themselves from them, as did the Roman philosopher Pliny the Elder (23–79 CE).[36] Women were commonly regarded as morally, intellectually, and spiritually inferior to men.

Consistent with the normal roles of men and women, Jesus chose men as his twelve primary disciples, but he had other followers or disciples, and some were women who were important enough to be mentioned by name in the New Testament. Among these were Mary Magdalene; Joanna the wife of "Herod's steward"; Mary the mother of Jesus; Mary the mother of James and John the sons of Zebedee; Salome, and "many others" who traveled with Jesus and his disciples from their home in Galilee to the Passover gathering in Jerusalem where he was killed (Mark 15:40–41, Luke 8:2–3, John 19:25). Near Jerusalem in Bethany, there were the sisters Martha and Mary; Jesus was said to have had a special love for them and their brother Lazarus (John 11:5). Mary of Bethany "sat at the Lord's feet and listened to his teaching," like a disciple, and Jesus commended her for this (Luke 10:38–42). In the story of the woman at the well (John 4), the disciples were surprised that Jesus talked with a Samaritan woman, and then she was the one who told the Samaritans about Jesus. In all four Gospels, the women were the ones who did not abandon Jesus at the cross. In the Gospels of John, Mark, and Luke, Mary Magdalene was the first to see the resurrected Jesus, and Jesus

---

33. Josephus, *Antiquities*, 4.8.15.

34. Josephus, *War* 2.8.2, *Antiquities* 18.1.5.

35. Philo of Alexandria, *Apology* 11.14–11.18.

36. Pliny the Elder, *Natural History*, V: 17, 4. For all three accounts of the Essenes (Josephus, Philo, and Pliny), see http://essene.com/History/AncientHistoriansAndEssenes.html

sent her to tell the news of his resurrection to his disciples—so she was a trusted messenger. True to the culture of the times, the disciples did not believe Mary and the other women who told them Jesus had risen.

Paul, although not a disciple until after Jesus was gone, seems to have carried on this openness to women, at least in principle. For example, he wrote that there is "neither Jew nor Greek, neither slave nor free, neither male nor female, for you are all one in Christ" (Gal. 3:28). The example of slavery is instructive—Paul did not incite slaves to leave their masters, even though "in Christ" the slave and master are equal brothers (Phlm 16). Although Paul preached that the end was at hand, he did not encourage his followers to drop everything and follow him, as Jesus had done. Rather, he told them to stay where they were until the end comes, which would not be long (1 Cor. 7:17–31). His revolution was not about changing the current order; that was something that would be done by God. He took a similar attitude toward women. In principle they are equal to men, but the norms of society still apply and women need to stay in their place and not speak out in church (1 Cor. 14:34–36). Paul recognized some women as important leaders of the Christian community, but his sense of freedom in Christ did not completely overcome his sense of what was proper.

Christians today sometimes justify Paul's instructions to women to stay silent in church as something that made sense in his time and situation. This is an argument for cultural relativism as an explanation for things in the Bible that seem biased or inconsistent. So, when Paul argued that women should keep silent because that was the way it was done "in all the churches" (1 Cor.14:33–36), was this a case of cultural sensitivity on Paul's part? He used this cultural rationale when addressing questions about drinking wine or eating meat sacrificed to idols (Rom. 14, 1 Cor. 8–10). Our goal is not to exercise our personal liberties, he said, it is to lead others to believe in Christ, and we should curtail some liberties if that will help the gospel. The problem with this explanation is that Paul justified his biases and blind spots regarding women not by cultural sensitivity, but by timeless arguments that would apply regardless of culture. He thought God saw things the same way he did. In 1 Corinthians (14), Paul explained that "it is shameful for a woman to speak in church," and this is not a matter of choice but of "the word of God." To Paul it just did not seem proper for women to speak in church, but he appealed to God as the authority for this, not culture.

Similarly, Paul was offended by women with short or uncovered hair (as in some cultures today that require covering for women), and by men with long hair (1 Cor. 11:3–16). This dress code might make sense if the reason for it were cultural—let's not offend people unnecessarily, Paul might say—but that was not the reason he gave. He said it is a disgrace for a woman to have her head uncovered, and that this is as bad as if her hair were cut short, perhaps referring to a practice of cutting the hair to shame an adulteress. He did not recognize that this was a matter of cultural perception, that it is not universally shameful for a woman to have short or uncovered hair. His arguments were based on absolute statements that would apply regardless of culture: (1) A man should not cover his head because he is the image and reflection of God, while a woman should cover her head because she is the reflection of the man; (2) "Nature itself" supports long hair on a woman and short hair on a man (an argument that seems contrary to fact); and (3) women should be covered "because of the angels," a cryptic statement that might have something to do with angels lusting after women as described in Genesis 6:2. None of these rationalizations made any real sense. What comes through loud and clear is that Paul thought women should be covered, but he could not see that this was a cultural bias. He appealed to some standard ideas about women: Men were created in the image of God, but women were created for men (referring to Genesis 2); anybody can see that a woman with her head uncovered is shameful, and so on. It was normal and human for Paul to have these cultural biases, but he wanted his sense of propriety to be divinely justified.

One interesting thing about this discussion of head covering is that Paul allowed a woman to pray or prophesy in church, as long as she was properly covered (1 Cor. 11:5). This has led some scholars to suggest that the passage in 1 Corinthians 14 saying "it is shameful for a woman to speak in church" may be a later interpolation and not actually written by Paul. The text flows better if the reference to women not speaking in church is removed, and it is well known that scribes sometimes inserted passages into texts as they were copied.[37] For example, margin notes by one copyist sometimes were included in the body of the text by another. My assessment is that these probably were Paul's words. He made an exception for women speaking in the Spirit (praying or prophesying), consistent with his belief that they could have the Spirit of God the same as men, but he did not allow women to address the church as teachers or in discussion because that offended his sense of what was proper. No doubt there are many people in the world today who would agree with him. I am reminded of a friend who told me she did not want to vote for a

---

37. Ehrman, *Misquoting Jesus*, ch. 2, 183–86; Ehrman, *Orthodox Corruption of Scripture*.

certain woman running for President of the United States, simply because she thought the president should not be a woman.

Whatever Paul's actual views on how women ought to cover their heads or speak in church, it is clear that he offered God's salvation through belief in Jesus Christ to everyone, as there is "no male nor female" but we are "all one in Christ" (Gal. 3:28). In the letter to the Philippians (4:3), Paul described two women, Euodia and Syntyche, as "fellow workers," who "have labored side by side with me in the gospel . . . whose names are in the book of life." In the letter to the Romans (16:1–3) he described a woman, Phoebe, as "a deaconess of the church," and greeted Prisca (or Priscilla) before her husband Aquila as "fellow workers in Christ Jesus" who "risked their necks for my life." Priscilla is also named in the Acts of the Apostles as one who with her husband Aquila expounded the Christian message to Apollos, who became a prominent apostle (Acts 18:26, 1 Cor. 3:4–5). Junia, mentioned by Paul as prominent among the apostles (Rom. 16:7), was also a female name.[38]

Taking all of these examples together, it seems that Paul was open to women having a prominent place in the Christian community and recognized some as leaders, but he had some conventional ideas about how they ought to dress and act, and was not above equating his cultural biases with timeless spiritual truths. In 1 Timothy, one of the latest books in the New Testament, there is evidence that not everyone shared this openness to women, as more traditional and restrictive attitudes are evident in this book. There are several reasons for thinking Paul did not write this letter despite its claim that he did, and this is one of those reasons. Other reasons include the Greek writing style and vocabulary, and the discussion of a formal church hierarchy that did not exist in the time of Paul.[39] The author of 1 Timothy instructed women to adorn themselves modestly, not with braided hair or jewels but with good deeds, "as befits women who profess religion," and continued:

> Let a woman learn in silence with all submissiveness. I permit no woman to teach or to have authority over men; she is to keep silent. For Adam was formed first, then Eve; and Adam was not deceived, but the woman was deceived and became a transgressor. Yet a woman will be saved through bearing children, if she continues in faith and love and holiness, with modesty. (1 Tim. 2:11–15)

38. The Revised Standard Version changed the female name Junia to the male Junias, and added the word "men" to the sentence, a case where the King James Version may be a more accurate translation.

39. Ehrman, *New Testament*, ch. 24.

The first part of this passage in 1 Timothy is not much different from 1 Corinthians (14:34–36), that "women should keep silent in the churches," but the last sentence is far from the teaching of Paul that everyone, man or woman, is saved through faith in Jesus Christ. If women are saved through childbearing, then Paul would not have urged both men and women to remain unmarried "for the time is growing short" (1 Cor. 7), and he would not have said that there is no male nor female in Christ (Gal. 3:28). According to Paul, women will be saved through faith in Christ, the same as men. It is hard to imagine the Paul of Romans, Galatians, or 1 Corinthians saying anything like this verse in 1 Timothy.

This passage from 1 Timothy based the silencing and suppression of women not on cultural sensitivity, but on a universal and timeless argument drawn from the story of Adam and Eve. By this way of thinking, women are spiritually and morally inferior to men but they can be saved if they are modest, righteous, holy, and bear children. It calls to mind the curse pronounced when Adam and Eve were cast out of the Garden of Eden, that women would have travail in childbirth and be dominated by men (Gen. 3:16). This is a traditional Jewish doctrine, but seems to contradict the teaching and practice of Paul and Jesus. This passage in 1 Timothy may reflect the stubborn persistence of social norms and biases even in the face of the declaration that there is no male and female in Christ, and that Christ has freed us from the curse of the sin of Adam and Eve (Rom. 5:17–21). This issue continued to be debated among Christians in the second century, as evidenced by the influential church leader Tertullian of Alexandria (about 200 CE). In a diatribe against people he considered heretics, he wrote: "The women of the heretics—how forward they are! They have the impudence to teach, to argue, to perform exorcisms and cures—they may even baptize!"[40] Clearly, Tertullian expected the reader to agree that these impudent actions of some Christian women are scandalous and must be stopped. His comments demonstrate that there were Christians with other ideas, who allowed women to be active participants and leaders in their churches.

FORGERIES AND ATTRIBUTIONS

I previously stated that 1 Timothy probably was not written by Paul, even though it names him as the author. Just as it is possible to distinguish

---

40. Tertullian, *Prescription Against Heretics*, 41, translation based on Ehrman, *After the New Testament*.

modern authors by differences in style, so Greek scholars have studied the vocabulary, style, and content of letters attributed to Paul, to judge the likelihood that the same person wrote them all. This concept may come as a surprise to people who assume he wrote everything with his name on it, but there are good reasons to be suspicious of authorship claims.[41] In ancient times, authors often used the name of a famous person to give their writing more weight, or they may have felt they were honoring a mentor by writing in his name. Perhaps some of the epistles of Paul were written by his disciples who were carrying on his work. Historians of the New Testament generally agree that Romans, 1 and 2 Corinthians, Galatians, Philippians, 1 Thessalonians and Philemon were written by Paul. Titus and 1 and 2 Timothy probably were not written by Paul, for reasons of style, doctrine (such as the assertion that women will be saved through bearing children), and the presumption of a church hierarchy (bishops, etc.) that did not exist in Paul's time. Many scholars also conclude that Paul did not write Ephesians or Colossians. These two letters have Paul's usual emphasis on the Holy Spirit, but the characteristic focus on the return of Christ is missing. Paul typically sees salvation and resurrection as things that will happen in the future when Christ returns (e.g., Rom. 5:9, 6:4, 13:11), but in these letters Christian believers are already saved and symbolically resurrected through faith (Eph. 2:5, Col. 2:12). Ephesians and Colossians may be examples of the shift in Christian thinking from the future to the present in the generation after Paul, as the expected end did not arrive.

The authorship of 2 Thessalonians is a matter of much debate. It conveys less urgency about the coming end than does 1 Thessalonians, but the difference can be explained as a change in emphasis to address a different situation. Either way, 2 Thessalonians demonstrates the fact that forged letters did exist, for the writer said he did not want the Thessalonians to be alarmed by a letter "purporting to be from us" saying that the Day of the Lord had already come (2 Thess. 2:2). Apparently, someone had written a letter claiming to be from Paul saying that the expected return of Christ had happened, and this caused a stir in the Thessalonian church. Paul (if the author was Paul) wrote to reassure them that the letter was a fake, and some things still had to happen before the end. Thus there is evidence in the New Testament itself that pseudonymous letters were in circulation, and it appears that some made it into the Bible. The books of the New Testament

---

41. Ehrman, *New Testament*, ch. 23.

are among the earliest Christian writings still in existence, but they were not all written by the authors they claim.[42]

In addition to the letters that claim Paul as author, there are other books in the New Testament attributed to prominent apostles. The Epistle to the Hebrews traditionally has been attributed to Paul on the basis of the closing that is in his style, but the book as a whole is very different from Paul's usual writing. The Epistle of James was attributed to James the brother of Jesus and leader of the Jerusalem Christians, and this probably accounts for its inclusion in the New Testament. The letter begins, "James, a servant of God and of the Lord Jesus Christ" (James 1:1), but James was a very common name. There are at least four "James" named in the New Testament: James the brother of Jesus (Mark 6:3), James the son of Zebedee (Matt. 4:21), James the son of Alphaeus (Matt. 10:3), and James the father of Judas (Luke 6:16). There is no mention of a family connection to Jesus in the Epistle of James, no mention of any details of the life or teachings of Jesus, and nothing of James as a witness of the resurrection of Jesus (1 Cor. 15:7) In fact, the letter hardly mentions Jesus at all. There is a list of examples of great acts of faith, but they are all from the Old Testament, none from the life of Jesus or his disciples. There is no reason other than pious tradition to think this book was written by James the brother of Jesus. The doctrinal content of the book is consistent with what is known of James as a leader of Jewish Christians, which may account for its attribution to him, but it might as well be anonymous for all we know of the author.

The New Testament also contains three letters attributed to "John", as well as the Revelation of John, all traditionally connected to the prominent disciple of Jesus, John the son of Zebedee. Like James, John was a very common name, and these writings make no claim to have been written by one of the twelve disciple of Jesus. Except for the Revelation of John, they do not name the author at all. Biblical historians generally agree that the three epistles were connected to the same group that produced the Gospel of John, which was also anonymous. Even if these writings were authored by someone named John, there is no reason to believe they were written by John of the twelve disciples, and some good reasons to think they were not. John the son of Zebedee was a peasant fisherman from Galilee and a speaker of Aramaic, not Greek, the language of these books. Even if he knew Greek, he is described in the book of Acts as uneducated and may have

---

42. For discussion of the authorship of books of the New Testament, see Harris, *New Testament*; Ehrman, *New Testament*.

been illiterate (Acts 4:13). His brother James was killed by Herod Antipas (son of Herod the Great, Acts 12:2), and John may also have been killed around that time, as he dropped from the story after playing a prominent role in the beginning (Acts 3, Gal. 2:9). As with the Epistle of James, there is nothing in the letters of John that would indicate the author knew Jesus personally. Christians have just assumed that these and other books were written by their famous namesakes.

The New Testament contains two letters attributed to Simon Peter, leader of the twelve disciples of Jesus. Peter was also a leader of the Christians in Jerusalem, along with John the son of Zebedee, and James the brother of Jesus. Later, according to tradition, he was leader of the Christians in Rome and was martyred there in 64 CE. There is broad agreement among historians that 2 Peter was one of the latest books in the New Testament to be written, and was not written or dictated by the apostle Peter. For one thing, 2 Peter mentions the letters of Paul as being in circulation among Christians (2 Peter 3:15–16), so it must have been written well after these other letters. Also, there is nothing in it that would indicate it came from someone who was an actual disciple of Jesus except for a reference to the transfiguration of Jesus, a story that could have come from one of the Gospels.

There were many other writings outside the Bible falsely attributed to this famous apostle, but the epistle of 1 Peter in the New Testament is the only book that some historians consider as possibly authored by Peter. Like John, Peter was a peasant fisherman who spoke Aramaic, and probably was illiterate (Acts 4:13). He could have dictated to someone who wrote the letter in Greek, but the use of many quotes from the Septuagint (the Greek translation of the Jewish scriptures) suggest an educated, Greek-speaking Jew as the author, not a peasant fisherman. Furthermore, like 2 Peter and the epistles of John and James, there is nothing in the letter that would suggest the author actually walked with Jesus as his intimate disciple, or was a primary witness of his resurrection. Finally, 1 Peter reflects a time when Christians were spread throughout Asia Minor and were widely persecuted (1 Peter 1:1), another indication that it was written after the time of Peter, perhaps in the late first century CE. For these reasons, it is unlikely that the apostle Peter actually wrote either of the epistles attributed to him in the New Testament. As historical sources, the primary value of the epistles of Peter, James and John is as witnesses to the beliefs, concerns and practices of some early Christians, as Christianity grew and spread and became a religion separate from its Jewish roots.

5

Filled with the Holy Spirit

The Holy Spirit of God as an active presence in the world is a dominant theme in the New Testament. In the Acts of the Apostles, probably written by the same author as the Gospel of Luke, the defining characteristic of Christian believers is that they are filled with the Holy Spirit, giving them spiritual power (Luke 24:49, Acts 1:5, 2:1–43, 10:47, 11:16–18). This is what brings the promise of God's kingdom already in the lives of believers, even as they wait for the end that will soon come. Similarly, in the Gospel of John it is the Comforter or Counselor who brings the presence of God, teaching and guiding as Jesus did, empowering us to be like him (John 14:15–27, 15:9–12, 16:7–15). This Comforter is also called "the Spirit of Truth" and identified as "the Holy Spirit":

> [Jesus said] I will pray the Father, and he will give you another Counselor, to be with you for ever, even the Spirit of truth, whom the world cannot receive, because it neither sees him nor knows him; you know him, for he dwells with you, and will be in you. I will not leave you desolate; I will come to you. Yet a little while, and the world will see me no more, but you will see me; because I live, you will live also. In that day you will know that I am in my Father, and you in me, and I in you.
> . . . the Counselor, the Holy Spirit, whom the Father will send in my name, he will teach you all things, and bring to your remembrance all that I have said to you. (John 14:16–20, 26 RSV)

The phrase "Holy Spirit," sometimes translated "Holy Ghost," is literally the sacred breath, or breath of God. The Greek word *pneuma* meant both the physical breath as well as the life spirit of a person. The Spirit of God first appears in the Bible in the story of creation, when "the spirit [wind or breath] of God moved upon the waters" (Gen. 1:2). In a vision related by the prophet Ezekiel, it was this divine breath or wind that restored life to a pile of bones that symbolized the people of Israel (Ezek. 37). The Spirit of God is the agent of God in the world, and the source of prophecies and revelations. For example, in the story of Saul, the first King of Israel, the prophet Samuel directed Saul to join a group of prophets where the Spirit of God would come upon him:

> . . . you will meet a band of prophets coming down from the high place with harp, tambourine, flute, and lyre before them, prophesying. Then the spirit of the Lord will come mightily upon you, and you shall prophesy with them and be turned into another man. Now when these signs meet you, do whatever your hand finds to do, for God is with you. (1 Sam. 10:5–7, RSV)

What was this "prophesying"? Prophesying in the Bible usually involved speaking for God. The Spirit of God in these stories is contagious, and when it comes upon a person they cannot help but prophesy, even against their will (1 Sam. 19:18–24). The book of the prophet Joel says that when the Day of the Lord comes and Israel is restored, God will "pour out his spirit," giving prophecies and visions (Joel 2:27–32). These and similar passages may have been on the minds of the followers of Jesus who believed they had received the Holy Spirit through faith in Christ.

In the New Testament, the Gospel of Luke tells the story of the Jewish prophet John the Baptist, "filled with the Holy Ghost even from his mother's womb" (Luke 1:15). His father and mother were both described as "filled with the Holy Spirit" at times, inspiring them to prophesy (Luke 1:41, 67). The Holy Spirit was described as "resting upon" a righteous man named Simeon who had been told by the Spirit that the Messiah would come in his lifetime (Luke 2:25–27). In both accounts of the virgin birth, it was the Holy Spirit who was responsible for Mary's pregnancy with Jesus (Matt. 1:18–20; Luke 1:35). These stories recall the role of the Spirit of God in the Old Testament as God's agent in the world.

As an adult, John the Baptist foretold one who would come after him who would "baptize with the Holy Spirit" (Mark 1:8; Matt. 3:11). When Jesus was baptized by John, the Spirit of God descended upon him in the form of a dove. Jesus was "full of the Holy Spirit" (Luke 4:1) and he was led by this Spirit as he began his prophetic work (Matt. 4:1; Mark 1:12). In the Gospel of John and the Acts of the Apostles, after the resurrection of

Jesus the Holy Spirit was given to his disciples, but there are two different versions of how this happened.

According to the Gospel of John, after his death and resurrection Jesus delivered the Holy Spirit to the disciples directly:

> Jesus said to them again, "Peace be with you. As the Father has sent me, even so I send you." And when he had said this, he breathed on them, and said to them, "Receive the Holy Spirit. If you forgive the sins of any, they are forgiven; if you retain the sins of any, they are retained." (John 20:21–23, RSV)

Thus, Jesus embodied the Holy Spirit (breath of God), and he gave it directly to his chosen disciples. In the Gospel of John, this also seems to have been a transfer of authority, giving the disciples power to forgive sins. It is unclear how the Holy Spirit would come to the rest of us; perhaps it was to be passed on by these leaders.

In the Gospel of Luke and the Acts of the Apostles, the disciples were instructed by the risen Jesus to wait in Jerusalem where they would receive the Holy Spirit "from on high" (Luke 24:49). This would be the "baptism with the Holy Ghost" promised by John the Baptist (Acts 1:5–8). Soon after this, on the Jewish holy day of Pentecost, the Holy Spirit came to them "as a mighty, rushing wind," they spoke in languages they did not know, and they were emboldened to spread the gospel (Acts 2). Peter on this occasion quoted the prophet Joel and said these events were a sign of the time of the end, when God would "pour out his spirit on all flesh," and that this promise of the Holy Spirit is to all who believe:

> This is what was spoken by the prophet Joel, and in the last days it shall be, God declares, that "I will pour out my Spirit upon all flesh, and your sons and your daughters shall prophesy, and your young men shall see visions, and your old men shall dream dreams; yea, and on my menservants and my maidservants in those days I will pour out my Spirit; and they shall prophesy. And I will show wonders in the heaven above and signs on the earth beneath, blood, and fire, and vapor of smoke; the sun shall be turned into darkness and the moon into blood, before the day of the Lord comes, the great and manifest day. And it shall be that whoever calls on the name of the Lord shall be saved." (Acts 2:16–21, RSV, quoting Joel 2:28–32)

According to this version of events, after this "baptism with the Holy Spirit," the disciples were empowered to perform signs and wonders as Jesus did and many people joined the group of believers. Later, it was this same experience of the Holy Spirit "falling" on a group of non-Jews (who then spoke in tongues) that convinced Peter and others that the gospel of Jesus Christ was not just for Jews, but for anyone who believes (Acts 10:44–48, 11:15–19).

The apostle Paul emphasized the Holy Spirit as the essential difference between those who are "in Christ" and those who are not. According to Paul, after he came to believe in Jesus Christ he received the Holy Spirit, and it is this Spirit who works in all who believe to do the work of God (Acts 2:17; 1 Cor. 2:12; Gal. 3:2–3). This Spirit of God raised Christ from the dead, and is performing a similar work in believers to raise them up in a mystical sense in this life and the life to come (Rom. 8).

Paul, by his own account, had been converted through an experience of the risen Jesus that turned him from persecuting Christians to joining them (Gal. 1:11–17, Acts 22:1–21). Paul believed that the Spirit of God was active in the community of believers through spiritual gifts such as healing, prophecy (speaking for God through the Spirit), speaking in tongues, revelations, and divine guidance (for example, 1 Cor. 2, 12, 14). He said, "All who are led by the Spirit of God are the sons of God," and "the Spirit himself bears witness with our spirit that we are the children of God" (Rom. 8:14–16). He emphasized that by living in the Spirit and having "the mind" of Christ (Phil. 2:1–5) we will do the things that God wants us to do freely, fulfilling the law of Moses:

> For you were called to freedom, brethren; only do not use your freedom as an opportunity for the flesh, but through love be servants of one another. For the whole law [of Moses] is fulfilled in one word, "You shall love your neighbor as yourself." But if you bite and devour one another take heed that you are not consumed by one another. But I say, walk by the Spirit, and do not gratify the desires of the flesh . . . if you are led by the Spirit you are not under the law.
>
> . . . the fruit of the Spirit is love, joy, peace, patience, kindness, goodness, faithfulness, gentleness, self-control; against such there is no law.
>
> And those who belong to Christ Jesus have crucified the flesh with its passions and desires. If we live by the Spirit, let us also walk by the Spirit. Let us have no self-conceit, no provoking of one another, no envy of one another. (Gal. 5:13–26, RSV)

Paul was convinced that the Holy Spirit would transform believers and unify them in love, faith, and service to God. By drawing near to God in the Spirit, we will understand God's will and know the truth, bringing us all together as "heirs of God and joint-heirs with Christ" (Rom. 8:17). In the letter to the Ephesians, this hope was summed up in a prayer, echoing Paul's typical focus on the transformative power of the Spirit, and the mystical love of Christ:

> I bow my knees before the Father . . . that according to the riches of his glory he may grant you to be strengthened with might through his Spirit in the inner man, and that Christ may dwell in your hearts through faith; that you, being rooted and grounded in love, may have power to comprehend with all the saints what is the breadth and length and height and depth, and to know the love of Christ which surpasses knowledge, that you may be filled with all the fullness of God. (Eph. 3:14–20, RSV)

In these examples from the Gospel of John, the Acts of the Apostles, and the teachings of Paul, the Holy Spirit is something that people receive through faith in Christ. The result is a change in the way a person thinks and lives, and a connection within the believer to the Spirit of God. After receiving the Holy Spirit, the believer is "in Christ," as "a new creation . . . old things have passed away; behold, all things have become new" (2 Cor. 5:17). This "new man" is "created after the likeness of God in true righteousness and holiness" (Eph. 4:24). This mystical experience of the Holy Spirit, the living presence of God in each person, is a central theme in the New Testament writings and a key to understanding their context and purpose.

6

The Message of the End—A Closer Look

SIGNS OF THE END

For the apostle Paul, life in the Holy Spirit was a foretaste of the glorious future when we would all be changed to live with Christ as the children of God in his everlasting kingdom. Paul wrote to the Roman Christians:

> You know what time it is, how it is full time now for you to awake from sleep. For salvation is nearer to us than when we first believed; the night is far gone, the day is at hand. (Rom. 13:11–12)

The urgency of Paul's message echoed the proclamation of the Gospels that the Kingdom of God is at hand (Mark 1:15).

In the synoptic Gospels, the saying of Jesus that no one knows the exact time of the end is coupled with the saying that it will happen in that generation, along with a description of the signs of the end. These signs include the desecration and destruction of the temple, a time of great tribulation such as the world has never seen, and signs in the heavens when the "Son of Man" finally comes in power to gather his chosen ones. Given the importance of these sayings to the followers of Jesus then and in modern times, it is worth considering them in detail, quoted here from the Gospel of Mark:

> And as he sat on the Mount of Olives opposite the temple, Peter and James and John and Andrew asked him privately, "Tell us, when will this be [the destruction of the temple], and what will be the sign when these things are all to be accomplished?"
>
> And Jesus said to them . . . "When you hear of wars and rumors of wars, do not be alarmed; this must take place, but the end

is not yet. For nation will rise against nation, and kingdom against kingdom; there will be earthquakes in various places, there will be famines; this is but the beginning of the birth-pangs.

But take heed to yourselves; for they will deliver you up to councils; and you will be beaten in synagogues; and you will stand before governors and kings for my sake, to bear testimony before them.

And the gospel must first be preached to all nations.

. . . he who endures to the end will be saved.

But when you see the desolating sacrilege set up where it ought not to be (let the reader understand), then let those who are in Judea flee to the mountains . . .

For in those days there will be such tribulation as has not been from the beginning of the creation which God created until now, and never will be . . .

But in those days, after that tribulation, the sun will be darkened, and the moon will not give its light, and the stars will fall from heaven, and the powers in the heavens will be shaken. And then they will see the Son of Man coming in clouds with great power and glory. And then he will send out the angels, and gather his elect from the four winds, from the ends of the earth to the ends of heaven. From the fig tree learn its lesson: as soon as its branch becomes tender and puts forth its leaves, you know that summer is near. So also, when you see these things taking place, you know that he is near, at the very gates.

Truly, I say to you, *this generation will not pass away before all these things take place.* Heaven and earth will pass away, but my words will not pass away.

But of that day or that hour no one knows, not even the angels in heaven, nor the Son, but only the Father. Take heed, watch; for you do not know when the time will come. (Mark 13:5–7, 19, 24–34, RSV, emphasis added)

As a Christian centuries later, I studied this and similar passages to understand what would happen in the time of the end. Given the restoration of the state of Israel, the rise of a global society, and the ability of people to destroy themselves with nuclear weapons, I, like many Christians, thought I might be living in that time. I assumed that Jesus was talking to the people of the end time, maybe even me, but not the people standing right in front of him. This passage encourages this interpretation, as it warns several times that we must be patient and endure. It will take some time to preach the gospel to all nations, and there will be a time of persecution before the end. Jesus speaks as if he will not be there when all this happens. Luke added that "the times of the gentiles" must be fulfilled, while Jews are led captive among the nations, probably a reference to the destruction of Jerusalem and the fact that the Romans were still in charge (Luke 21:24). All of this suggests that Jesus was sending a message to believers some time later.

What was the intent of the people who wrote these words of Jesus in the Gospel of Mark, and the other Gospels that include these and similar sayings? With hindsight that the end did not happen during the decades since Jesus, the Gospel writers naturally thought some time had to elapse first. No one knows the day or the hour, they said, but they still thought the end had to be soon, in their generation—and the crisis in Jerusalem in 70 CE was one of the signs. Mark was saying, "Jesus knew it would not happen right away, but now with the fall of Jerusalem it really is happening, see the signs!" Many Christians of the late first century, with the destruction of the temple and the persecution of Christians, thought they were experiencing the "birth pangs" prophesied by Jesus himself, and their writings reflected that belief, decades after Jesus actually said the words. This is why the synoptic Gospels have a sense of urgency, but also say that Jesus did not mean it would happen immediately. The writers believed it was happening several decades after Jesus, in their time.

The apostle Paul emphasized different things about this in his two letters to the Thessalonians. In 1 Thessalonians (probably the earliest book in the New Testament) he said the Day of the Lord could happen any time, catching people by surprise, "like a thief in the night" (1 Thess. 5:2). However, in 2 Thessalonians he said that some things must happen first. One of the signs of the end would be the desecration of the Jerusalem Temple (2 Thess. 2:3–4), as Jesus predicted in the Gospel of Mark ("the desolating sacrilege," Mark 13:14). This reference to the temple by both Mark and Paul shows a common understanding among Christians about the events of the end that included the desecration of the temple as an important sign. "Watch for the signs," they said, because the end will come suddenly "like a thief in the night."

Why did Mark drop a hint about "the desolating sacrilege," saying "let the reader understand" (Mark 13:14)? The suggestion is that there is something we all should recognize, and maybe it has already happened or looks likely to happen soon. Jews in the time of Jesus remembered that the temple had been violated more than a century earlier, when the Syrian king Antiochus IV (reigned 175–163 BCE) took the temple treasures, erected a statue of the Greek god Zeus in the temple, and sacrificed "unclean" animals (such as pigs) on the temple altars.[1] These attempts to insult and eradicate the Jewish religion resulted in a revolt that eventually brought the temple back into Jewish control, events that are celebrated during the festival of Hanukkah. The Jewish scripture 1 Maccabees (1:54, 6:7) described this desecration of the temple with words similar to those of the Gospels, often translated "abomination of desolation" (Matt. 24:15), or "desolating sacrilege."

Something like this invasion of the temple is what the New Testament writers thought would happen at the time of the end. Less than a decade after Jesus, the temple was threatened by the Roman Emperor Caligula, who reigned 37–41 CE. Caligula commanded that all should worship him, and that a statue of himself (as Zeus) be erected in the Jerusalem temple. This almost led to a Jewish uprising but Caligula was assassinated and the order was cancelled.[2] The threat became a reality when Jerusalem was besieged and finally destroyed three decades later. No wonder the temple was on the minds of Jews and Christians who were looking for the signs of the end. The destruction of the temple was one of the most important signs that the Day of the Lord had arrived, and for them it was a concrete reality.

These prophecies of signs before the coming of "the Son of Man" were not created out of nothing by Jesus or his followers.[3] The Old Testament prophet Daniel was a primary source for predictions of a time of tribulation, desecration of the temple (Dan. 11:31, 12:11), resurrection of the dead (Dan. 12:1–2), an eternal Kingdom of God and his saints, and the Messiah as a powerful divine being called "Son of Man" (Dan. 7:11–22). The prophet Joel foretold the restoration of Israel accompanied by signs in the heavens, "the sun turned to darkness and the moon turned to blood before the great and terrible day of the Lord" (Joel 2:31).

These ideas were part of the Jewish apocalyptic milieu of the time of Jesus. They were present in the Dead Sea Scrolls,[4] and in the book of Enoch,[5] which was not included in the Bible but was regarded as sacred scripture by some Jews and early Christians. Enoch was quoted in the New Testament

---

1. Harris, *New Testament*, 52–53; Schiffman, *Understanding Second Temple and Rabbinic Judaism*, ch. 3; Newsome, *Greeks, Romans, Jews*, ch. 1, 2.

2. Josephus, *Antiquities* 18.8.2–6, 8; Ehrman, *Jesus: Apocalyptic Prophet*, 117.

3. Ehrman, *Jesus: Apocalyptic Prophet*, 145–48; Newsome, *Greeks, Romans, Jews*, 66–101, 240–47; Schiffman, *Reclaiming the Dead Sea Scrolls*, ch. 19.

4. Schiffman, *Reclaiming the Dead Sea Scrolls*, 341–44.

5. G.E. Nickelsburg, "First and Second Enoch," ch. 5 in Levine et al., *Historical Jesus*; Ehrman, *Jesus, Apocalyptic Prophet*, 144–48.

(Jude 14–15, 1 Enoch 1:9), describing how the Messiah will come with ten thousand of his holy ones to execute judgment on the wicked. Using these familiar concepts, Jesus and Paul were consistent with their culture in their predictions of signs before the final events of the end. They added a sense of urgency that all this would come quickly in their time. There will be signs, but the end will come quickly and will take people by surprise.

It is likely that the need for some things to happen first received greater emphasis as time went on and urgent expectations were disappointed. This may be one explanation for some apparent differences between warnings of an event that might catch us sleeping, versus those that say the end will be announced by signs. In modern times, many Christians have said there will be two events marking the return of the Lord, the first being "the Rapture" that could happen any moment, and the second being the final Day of the Lord. This idea of two separate events, separated by a period of tribulation and signs, did not show up in Christian writings until after the Protestant Reformation more than sixteen centuries after the New Testament was written.

THE SON OF MAN

Jesus said the "Son of Man" will come in the clouds with power and great glory (Mark 13:26). This is based on the prophet Daniel, who described a heavenly being he saw in a vision as "like a son of man," meaning simply that the being looked like a human, as when God addressed the prophet Ezekiel as "son of man" (Ezek. 2:1). This and other prophecies grew together into the idea of a coming Messiah, called the Son of Man, who would restore Israel as God's eternal kingdom on earth:

> I saw in the night visions, and behold, with the clouds of heaven there came one like a son of man, and he came to the Ancient of Days and was presented before him. And to him was given dominion and glory and kingdom, that all peoples, nations, and languages should serve him; his dominion is an everlasting dominion, which shall not pass away, and his kingdom one that shall not be destroyed. (Dan. 7:13–14, RSV)

Thus, to apocalyptic Jews the phrase "son of man" had a double meaning.[6] It could mean a human being, but by the time of Jesus, "Son of Man" also had become a title for the powerful figure described by Daniel,

---

6. Ehrman, *Jesus, Apocalyptic Prophet*, 144–48; Levine and Brettler, *Jewish Annotated New Testament*, 545–46.

equated with the Messiah. This title is found outside the New Testament in the book of Enoch,[7] for example: "pain shall seize them when they see the Son of Man sitting on the throne of his glory" (1 Enoch 62:5; cf. Matt. 19:28, 24:30). Sayings of Jesus about the end time often referred to this Son of Man, as in the passage quoted previously from Mark (13). It is unclear whether or not Jesus was referring to himself when he used this title.[8] Nevertheless, it is clear that his disciples who spread the message of his resurrection believed that was exactly who he was, and that he would return on the clouds of heaven with power and glory, the divine and powerful Son of Man of Daniel and Enoch. These Jewish followers of Jesus were well within their time and culture with these beliefs, and were unusual only in that they believed Jesus was the fulfillment of the promise that they and other Jews desperately hoped for.

THE DESTRUCTION OF JERUSALEM

According to the historian Josephus, who was an eyewitness, the apocalyptic fervor of Jewish militants grew to a climax when they took control of Jerusalem and the Roman army surrounded the city in 66–70 CE.[9] Surely this was the time when God would intervene on behalf of his people, they hoped and prayed. Christians recalled that Jesus had foretold the destruction of the Jerusalem temple, and that the time of the end would be a time of wars and persecution before the salvation of God. The community on the shore of the Dead Sea, who produced the Dead Sea Scrolls, also believed that the existing temple was defiled and would be replaced by a new divine temple.[10] They had elaborate plans and prophecies for how the final battle would play out, written in their scrolls. It was perhaps the realization that things were not working out as they had planned that led them to hide the scrolls in caves for safekeeping, to be found almost 1900 years later. When Jerusalem was destroyed in 70 CE and the Messiah did not show up, the central authority and organization of both Judaism and Christianity were greatly weakened, and these sister religions entered a new phase in their history. For Jews, leadership shifted to local rabbis and synagogues, and the annual pilgrimages and

---

7. Newsome, *Greeks, Romans, Jews*, 85.

8. Ehrman, *New Testament*, 251–53; 278–79.

9. Josephus, *War*, 4.6.3, 2.22.1

10. Barrett, *New Testament Background*, 246; Schiffman, *Qumran and Jerusalem*, 96; Schiffman, *Reclaiming the Dead Sea Scrolls*, ch. 16, 20, 24.

animal sacrifices in Jerusalem ended.[11] Christianity gradually became a more gentile religion and moved away from its Jewish roots, with centers emerging in Rome, Antioch, and Alexandria. It was probably during this time in the late first century CE that the four Gospels were written, compiled from various sources, the authors collecting and interpreting the stories and teachings of Jesus as they had been passed on by his followers. The New Testament reflects the confusion of this time, the strong apocalyptic fervor that surrounded the destruction of Jerusalem, and continued hope in God in the present even as the hope of the Kingdom of Heaven on earth was deferred.

---

11. Schiffman, *Understanding Second Temple and Rabbinic Judaism*; Levine, *The Misunderstood Jew.*

7

Lost Scriptures and the New Testament

DEAD SEA SCROLLS, NAG HAMMADI, AND CHRISTIAN DIVERSITY

There were many books that Christians valued as inspired scripture, some attributed to the founding apostles, but not all of them ended up in the New Testament. Due to the popularity of novels and movies such as *The Da Vinci Code*,[1] many people have heard that writings such as the Dead Sea Scrolls or the gnostic gospels of Nag Hammadi give the true story of Jesus and his followers. I wish it were true that there is much information about the historical Jesus outside the Bible, but unfortunately this is fiction.

The Dead Sea Scrolls, discovered in 1947 in caves near the Dead Sea, were from the time and culture of Jesus but they had nothing to do with him directly, despite some early claims that they did.[2] It is likely that John the Baptist and Jesus were familiar with the community at Qumran that produced the scrolls, especially if it was connected with the Essenes who were described by Josephus as "in every city,"[3] but the scrolls tell us nothing about Jesus or John personally. Like the early Christians, the Qumran community expected the Messiah, an imminent apocalypse, and a new Kingdom of God, and they were critical of the administration of the Jerusalem temple.[4]

---

1. Brown, *Da Vinci Code*.

2. Schiffman, *Qumran and Jerusalem*, ch. 1, Schiffman, *Reclaiming the Dead Sea Scrolls*; P. Flint, "Jesus and the Dead Sea Scrolls," 110–31 in Levine et al., *Historical Jesus*.

3. Josephus, *Antiquities* 18.1.5.

4. P. Flint, "Jesus and the Dead Sea Scrolls," 110–31 in Levine et al., *Historical Jesus*; Schiffman, *Reclaiming the Dead Sea Scrolls*, ch. 20, 21.

Prior to the discovery of the scrolls, some historians assumed that some of the language in the Gospel of John and the epistles of John (1, 2 and 3 John) was an indication of later influences, and not part of the Jewish roots of Christianity. This included sayings about the sons of light or darkness, and those who are of the truth. The Dead Sea Scrolls showed that similar language was used by the Qumran community, and could have come from the original Jewish Christians, with no need for a later non-Jewish influence to explain it.[5] The scrolls also mentioned the legendary Old Testament priest Melchizedek (Gen. 14:18, Ps. 110:4), providing some context for references to Melchizedek in the book of Hebrews (Heb. 7).[6] The Dead Sea Scrolls are invaluable for understanding the culture of Jesus and his disciples, but do not tell us anything about Jesus himself.

The Nag Hammadi Library is a collection of documents dating from the fourth century CE in Egypt, buried in a pottery jar at that time and rediscovered in 1945.[7] These documents provide a wealth of sources from a branch of Christianity called gnosticism, but add almost nothing to our knowledge of the historical Jesus and his first disciples. The exception is the Gospel of Thomas, mentioned previously for its non-apocalyptic depiction of Jesus. Thomas may show the influence of gnostic ideas, but also appears to contain some early variations of Jesus' sayings that were transmitted independently of the New Testament Gospels. Thomas may even contain some authentic sayings of Jesus not found in the New Testament, for example:

> I have set a fire in the world, and behold, I am tending it until it blazes. (Thomas 10)

> Love your brother like your soul, guard him like the pupil of your eye. (Thomas 25)

> The kingdom of the Father is like a woman who was carrying a jar full of meal. While she was walking on a long road, the handle broke. The meal spilled behind her on the road but she did not notice. When she came to her house she set the jar down and found it empty. (Thomas 97)[8]

---

5. P. Flint, "Jesus and the Dead Sea Scrolls," 110–31 in Levine et al., *Historical Jesus*; Harris, *New Testament*, 190.

6. Harris, *New Testament*, 69, 324.

7. For the complete collection see Robinson, *Nag Hammadi Library*; For further discussion see Pagels, *Beyond Belief*; Ehrman, *Jesus: Apocalyptic Prophet*, 77.

8. Gospel of Thomas translations are from Meyer, *Secret Teachings of Jesus*; Ehrman, *Lost Scriptures*; Pagels, *Beyond Belief*.

The leadership of Jesus' brother James is mentioned in a cryptic passage in the Gospel of Thomas, suggesting a Jewish origin and ties with the Jewish-Christian followers of James in Jerusalem. He was sometimes called "James the Just" in early Christian writings:

> The disciples said to Jesus, "We know that you are going to leave us. Who will be our leader?" Jesus said to them, "Wherever you are, you are to go to James the Just, for whose sake heaven and earth came into being." (Thomas 12)

Identification with the poor as in the New Testament Gospels is found in Thomas, with familiar sayings such as "Blessed are the poor, yours is the Kingdom of Heaven" (Thomas 54). Also in Thomas is the parable of the king who had a banquet (Luke 14:15–24), but in Thomas it has a different twist as Jesus says the lesson is that "Business people and merchants will not enter the kingdom of my Father" (Thomas 64)! Regarding the role of women, Thomas contains sayings that place women on an equal standing with men as disciples of Jesus (Thomas 21, 22, 61, 114). Some sayings seem strangely unfamiliar and enigmatic, for example:

> Jesus said, "Be wanderers." (Thomas 42)

> If some say to you, 'Where have you come from?' Say to them, "We have come from the light, where the light came into being by itself . . . (Thomas 50)

> I am the light over all things, I am all: all came from me and all returns to me. Split a piece of wood and I am there, pick up a stone and you will find me there. (Thomas 75)

Of the four New Testament Gospels, John seems to be the closest to the Gospel of Thomas, as in these examples with the imagery of light and Jesus as the divine source of all things. John is also the Gospel in which the disciple Thomas figures most prominently, further suggesting the possibility of a connection between the two.[9] Although the personal relationship of each believer with Christ is important in both the New Testament and the Gospel of Thomas, in Thomas it is the light of God that is emphasized, rather than the Holy Spirit. The light was present at creation along with the divine word, when God said, "Let there be light," and there was light (Gen.

---

9. See Pagels, *Beyond Belief*, on possible links between the Gospels of Thomas and John.

1:3). This divine light preceded the creation of the sun or any other light, and so, like the divine word, represents the mystical source of all things.

The divine light also is identified as the source of enlightenment in the Gospel of John: "The true light that enlightens every man was coming into the world" (John 1:9; see also John 3:19–21). However, in the New Testament people do not have the Holy Spirit until they receive it through faith in Jesus Christ, who according to John was the embodiment of the divine light, the light of the world (John 8:12). In the Gospel of Thomas, the divine light is already present within a person, and Jesus reveals this. This "secret knowledge" (Greek *gnosis*) is the important thing, an aspect of Thomas that is similar to gnosticism. Consider the importance of "knowing yourself" in these sayings attributed to Jesus in the Gospel of Thomas:

> Those who seek should not stop seeking until they find. When they find, they will be disturbed. When they are disturbed, they will marvel, and will reign over all.
>
> If your leaders say to you, "Look, the (Father's) kingdom is in the sky," then the birds of the sky will precede you. If they say to you, "It is in the sea," then the fish will precede you. Rather, the kingdom is within you and it is outside you.
>
> When you know yourselves, then you will be known,[10] and you will understand that you are children of the living Father. But if you do not know yourselves, then you live in poverty, and you are the poverty. . . .
>
> Know what is in front of your face, and what is hidden from you will be disclosed to you. For there is nothing hidden that will not be revealed. (Thomas 2–5)

This saying that "the kingdom is within you" appears only once in the New Testament (Luke 17:20), but it appears twice in Thomas and is fundamental to the message. It also features prominently in another lost gospel, the Gospel of Mary, as follows:

> [Jesus, after his resurrection] greeted them all, saying, "Peace be with you. Receive my peace to yourselves. Beware that no one lead you astray saying 'Lo here!' or 'Lo there!' For *the Son of Man is within you. Follow after him!* Those who seek him will find him. Go then and preach the gospel of the kingdom. Do not lay down any rules beyond what I appointed you, and do not give a law like the lawgiver [Moses?] lest you be constrained by it." When he had said this He departed.

---

10. Cf. 1 Cor. 13:12.

But they were grieved. They wept greatly, saying, "How shall we go to the gentiles and preach the gospel of the kingdom of the Son of Man? If they did not spare him, how will they spare us?"

Then Mary stood up, greeted them all, and said to her brethren, "Do not weep and do not grieve nor be irresolute, for his grace will be entirely with you and will protect you. But rather let us praise his greatness, for he has prepared us and made us into men."

When Mary said this, she turned their hearts to the Good, and they began to discuss the words of the Savior. Peter said to Mary, "Sister, we know that the Savior loved you more than the rest of women. Tell us the words of the Savior which you remember which you know, but we do not, nor have we heard them."

Mary answered and said, "What is hidden from you I will proclaim to you."[11]

Mary then described a strange vision and conversation with Jesus, about the soul confronting various powers and reaching a place of eternal rest. Peter responded that this was a very strange teaching and he did not believe it came from the Savior. Peter said to the other disciples, "Did he really speak with a woman without our knowledge and not openly? Are we to turn about and all listen to her? Did he prefer her to us?" Mary then appealed to Peter that she was not lying, and Levi jumped in, saying:

"Peter, you have always been hot-tempered. Now I see you contending against the woman like the adversaries. But if the Savior has made her worthy, who are you indeed to reject her? Surely the Savior knows her very well. This is why he loved her more than us."

The Gospel of Mary reflected controversies in the early church about the role of women as leaders and teachers, and the legitimacy of visions and revelations. It advocated for unity among Christians, and asserted that Jesus had an important woman disciple who was at least the equal of Peter and the others. The depiction of Peter contrasts with the traditional doctrine that Peter was the rock on which the church was built, evidence of conflicts over church authority and Christian diversity that are well-documented from other sources of the time. The vision of Mary represents secret knowledge given only to her, an important theme in gnosticism that conflicted with efforts of some church leaders to exert control over doctrines and sources.[12]

---

11. Gospel of Mary translation by Ehrman, *Lost Scriptures*; see also Kirby, *Early Christian Writings*; Robinson, *Nag Hammadi Library*; Meyer, *Gospels of Mary*, ch. 2.

12. Pagels, *Beyond Belief*; Ehrman, *Lost Christianities*.

The Gospel of Mary, discovered in a fragment in Egypt in 1896, was probably written in Greek in the second century CE.[13] The disciple named Mary was most likely Mary Magdalene, or perhaps a conflation of Mary Magdalene and Mary of Bethany. These two Mary's who were disciples of Jesus have often been confused and combined in Christian tradition. The prominence of the disciple Mary in gnostic writings may result from the tradition that Mary Magdalene was the first witness of the resurrection (Matt. 28, Mark 16:9–11, John 20), and that Jesus had a special love for Mary of Bethany (as well as her brother Lazarus and sister Martha; John 11:1–5, Luke 10:39). The account of the resurrection in the Gospel of John, the Gospel often used by gnostics, portrayed a close personal relationship between Jesus and Mary, and she was entrusted by Jesus with the message of his resurrection to the rest of his disciples. There is no further mention in the New Testament of Mary Magdalene, Mary and Martha of Bethany, Mary the mother of Jesus, Salome or the other women mentioned in the Gospels, except that the mother of Jesus and "the women" were in Jerusalem with the other disciples after Jesus left them (Acts 1:14). There are conflicting traditions about what happened to these women. Their importance to early Christians is reflected in the memory of their names and their faithfulness in the Gospels, and the respect given to them by gnostics and other early Christians. The theologian Origen, in the third century CE, wrote that he had heard of Christian groups claiming to be followers of Salome, Mary, and Martha, but had not encountered these sects himself.[14]

Some sayings in the Gospel of Thomas probably reflect a gnostic influence, such as the opening statement: "these are the secret sayings that the living Jesus spoke and Judas Thomas the Twin wrote down" (Thomas 1). However, the extent to which Thomas was a product of gnostic thinking is a matter of ongoing debate.[15] Some common themes emerge among the other gnostic Christian writings in the Nag Hammadi collection[16] and related works such as the Gospel of Mary:

---

13. King, *Gospel of Mary of Magdala*.

14. Origen, *Against Celsus* 5:61; for the writings of Origen see Kirby, *Early Christian Writings*.

15. Ehrman, *Jesus: Apocalyptic Prophet*, ch. 5; Pagels, *Beyond Belief*.

16. Ehrman, *New Testament*, ch. 11; Ehrman, *Lost Christianities*, ch. 6; Pagels, *Gnostic Gospels*; the entire Nag Hammadi library, plus other related documents such as the Gospel of Mary, is available in Robinson, *Nag Hammadi Library*.

- These books do not claim to be about the life of Jesus. They offer the words of the risen Jesus, secret knowledge that he gave only to certain disciples, or that came in visions or revelations after his ascension. They are mystical, revelatory documents about the risen Christ.

- Gnostics generally downplayed or denied the humanity of Christ, or distinguished between the human Jesus and the eternal Christ. It was the eternal, divine Christ they were interested in, not the human Jesus. The deification of Christ to the point of denying his humanity was a broader trend in early Christianity, called docetism, of which the gnostics were an example.

- The gnostic gospels were not apocalyptic, and had an entirely different understanding of the world from that of the New Testament writers. The gnostic belief system may have predated Christianity as a branch of Jewish mysticism. Gnostics had a cosmic mythology and theology involving spiritual entities named Sophia and Seth, and they had a counterintuitive interpretation of Genesis that made the creator God a villain, trapping eternal spirits in bodies of flesh. Some gnostic writings seem to be a synthesis of gnostic and Christian beliefs, reinterpreting older gnostic writings.[17]

- The gnostic writings generally supported the idea of ongoing, secret revelations, sometimes reinterpreting verses from the Gospels or sayings of Jesus with new meanings. Gnostics believed they knew the correct and secret interpretations of the Jewish scriptures and the teachings of Jesus.

- Some gnostic writings placed a woman in a special position as the closest confidant of Jesus, usually Mary (probably referring to Mary Magdalene).[18] Thomas also played a special role as a hero, identified not only as "the twin" (Didymus) as in the Gospel of John (20:24), but as the actual twin brother of Jesus! Peter in the gnostic writings seems to represent Christians who are hostile to new revelations, secret teachings, and the leadership of women. Thomas and Mary know the secret teachings of Jesus, but Peter does not.

The main influence of the discovery of these documents on the study of Jesus has been a greater appreciation of the diversity of early Christians,

17. *Sophia of Jesus Christ, Apocryphon of John,* and *Treatise of the Great Seth* are examples of this synthesis.

18. These include *Gospel of Mary, Dialogue of the Savior, Gospel of Philip,* and *Pistis Sophia;* see Meyer, *Gospels of Mary.*

many of whom had beliefs different from those preserved in the New Testament tradition. They used the Gospels (especially John), and the writings of Paul, but they had their own writings as well. Gnostic Christians revered the risen Jesus as the source of revelations and mystical secrets through his living spirit. They thought they were the only ones who really understood what Jesus was about. There may be a reference to early gnostics in the New Testament, in a warning to "avoid the godless chatter and contradictions of what is falsely called knowledge [Greek *gnosis*]" (1 Tim. 6:20).

There were other versions of Christianity as well, such as Jewish Christians who strictly followed the laws of Moses. This was similar to the original version of Christianity led by Jesus' brother James (see chapter 9; Acts 15:1–21, 21:17–22; Gal. 1:18–19, 2:11–13). These Jewish Christians had their own writings instructing Christians to keep the Jewish laws, and they asserted the humanity of Jesus the Christ. This placed them on one end of the christological scale, with gnostics on the other denying the physical humanity of Christ.

Some other Christian writings available from the first few centuries after Jesus are romanticized stories of the apostles, or of other famous converts such as the woman Thecla who renounced marriage to follow Paul as a disciple. Some are fictional stories of Jesus as a miracle-working kid, or of Joseph and Mary (mother of Jesus) emphasizing Mary's holiness and perpetual virginity. Still others are pastoral letters written by church leaders. Some of these books were widely read and came close to making it into the final collection that became the New Testament.[19] They reveal much about how stories of Jesus and his disciples spread and changed, and what some people believed in the first centuries of Christianity as it became a Roman religion. They add little historical information about Jesus or his disciples beyond a few interesting but unverifiable traditions, such as the story that Thomas went to India (from the Acts of Thomas), or that Peter was crucified in Rome (from the Acts of Peter).[20]

ANTI-SEMITISM AND CELIBACY

Some early Christian writings argued for a particular interpretation of the Christian message, or polemicized against Jews, gnostics, or some other

19. Ehrman, *Lost Christianities*, ch. 5.

20. Sources for non-canonical early Christian writings include Ehrman, *Lost Scriptures*; Ehrman, *After the New Testament*; Cartlidge and Dungan, *Documents for the Study of the Gospels*; Kirby, *Early Christian Writings*.

group with whom the author disagreed. In the documents that have survived from the first few centuries of Christianity, there is a general trend toward anti-Semitism as Christianity became non-Jewish.[21] For example, the widely read Epistle of Barnabas (second century CE) said that Jews entirely misunderstood the true symbolic meaning of their own laws and scriptures. Christians argued over the meaning and relevance of the Jewish scriptures, and blamed the Jews for rejecting Jesus, even to the point of exonerating Pilate, the Roman official who actually ordered his execution. In one popular fictional account, Pilate wrote a letter apologizing to the Roman Emperor for killing the Son of God and King of the Jews, and blaming the Jews for his mistake. The Emperor (in this fictional story) issued a decree condemning the Jews for this crime, and naming this as the reason for the destruction of Jerusalem and exile of the Jews by the Romans. He condemned Pilate to death for failing to stop the execution of Jesus. Before Pilate died in this story, he prayed for forgiveness and salvation, and a voice from heaven answered, blessing him for his part in fulfilling the prophecies, and saying he will be a witness against the Jews at the Second Coming. When Pilate's head was chopped off an angel came down and carried his head to heaven (presumably his soul also went to heaven and not just his head!).[22]

There was another strong trend in early Christian writings toward the belief that sexual intercourse and reproduction are sinful or at least unholy and unspiritual. The idea that sex is inherently unholy is not present in Paul's discussion of marriage (1 Cor. 7), despite his support for celibacy, and Jews in general regarded procreation as a holy duty commanded by God (Gen. 1:28). Moses, the greatest Jewish prophet, was married, as were many of the other Old Testament prophets. Sex as unholy shows up in what is probably one of the latest books included in the New Testament, the book of Revelation. A vision of heaven describes 144,000 special ones who will be redeemed from the earth in the time of great tribulation before the end: "It is these who have not defiled themselves with women, for they are virgins" (Rev. 14:4). Virginity seems to be their most important qualification because it is listed first. In the Acts of Paul and Thecla, a popular early Christian book, the decision to follow Paul and Christ is equated with celibacy, as if marriage is a betrayal of faith in Christ.

---

21. Levine, *Misunderstood Jew.*

22. *A Letter from Pilate to Claudius,* translation by Cartlidge and Dungan, *Documents for the Study of the Gospels,* 82–84; See also Jensen, "How Pilate Became a Saint."

The growing antipathy toward sex in Christian writings may have been related to the fact that some influential early church leaders thought sex was unholy, and some were celibate. For example, Tertullian (about 200 CE) wrote that marriage is good and God created sex for procreation, but also described sexual relations as worthless, filthy and "an unseemly passion."[23] Tertullian cited Paul to argue that celibacy is better than marriage, but missed Paul's point that this was because he believed time was short and the end was near, not because sex is unholy (1 Cor. 7:26, 29). The Shepherd of Hermas, a book that was included in some early versions of the New Testament, opens with a passage that seems to equate any thought of sexual desire with sin.

The Acts of Thomas (not related to the Gospel of Thomas) made the unholiness of sex explicitly clear. In this story, a newlywed bride and groom (who happened to be royalty) narrowly escaped consummating their marriage and thereby ruining their lives and their chance to follow Jesus and please God. Jesus appeared on their wedding night in their bridal chamber (looking exactly like his twin brother Thomas, whom they had already met!) and told them:

> . . . know that if you refrain from this filthy intercourse you become temples holy and pure, being released from afflictions and troubles, known and unknown, and you will not be involved in the cares of life and of children, whose end is destruction . . .
>
> And you will be without care, spending an untroubled life . . . looking forward to receive that incorruptible and true marriage, and you will enter as groomsmen into that bridal chamber full of immortality and light.
>
> When the young people heard this, they believed the Lord and gave themselves over to him and refrained from filthy lust, and remained thus spending the night [in the bridal chamber].[24]

The next morning, the ecstatic newlyweds informed their parents of their new decision to forego sex and procreation, an announcement that was not well-received! The king and father of the bride was furious and tried to find Thomas, but he had already left for India.

This negative attitude toward sex and romanticizing of celibacy may reflect ascetic schools of Greek and Roman philosophy, such as stoicism and cynicism, that esteemed self-discipline, celibacy and control of

---

23. Tertullian, *To His Wife*, translation by Ehrman, *After the New Testament*, 399.

24. *Acts of Thomas* 12–13, translation by Ehrman, *Lost Scriptures*, 126.

passions. Some Roman religious cults excluded women and included vows of celibacy.[25] Pliny the Elder (23–79 CE), the Roman philosopher, praised celibacy in his description of the Essenes. Apollonius of Tyana (late first century CE), venerated in Roman temples as a divine healer and savior, was praised by his pious biographer for remaining celibate throughout his life, never marrying or participating in sexual pleasures:

> In this way he surpassed even Sophocles [the great philosopher] who said that he had escaped an uncontrollable and cruel master only when he had reached old age. But Apollonius through virtue and prudence was never overcome by lust even in his youth. Although he was still young, he controlled his bodily passion and completely mastered its mad craving.[26]

These examples show that this idea, that sexual passion is a sign of spiritual weakness and celibacy is virtuous, was common in Roman culture and was not invented by Christians. This attitude became embedded in Christianity and is the reason some people are scandalized by the idea that Jesus might have been married, or that his mother Mary had other children—if they were so holy this would be impossible, because, they believe, holy people are celibate almost by definition. In the Gospel of Matthew there is one passage where Jesus appears to say that it is better for a person to remain unmarried, but this is a special calling that not everyone can do:

> [Jesus said] "Whoever divorces his wife, except for unchastity, and marries another, commits adultery."
> The disciples said to him, "If such is the case of a man with his wife, it is not expedient to marry." But he said to them, "Not all men can receive this saying, but only those to whom it is given. . . . There are those who make themselves eunuchs for the sake of the kingdom of heaven." (Matt. 19:9–11, RSV)

In this exchange, the attitude portrayed is consistent with that of Paul, who encouraged people to be celibate so they could make the most of the little remaining time to prepare for the Kingdom of Heaven, "for the form of this world is passing away" (1 Cor. 7:31). Contrary to some later Christian writings, Paul actually advised that married people should not abstain from sex as a rule, to help them avoid temptations to adultery (1 Cor. 7:5). Paul also noted that, although he was unmarried, he had the right to be accompanied

---

25. Harris, *New Testament*, 44.

26. Flavius Philostratus, *The Life of Apollonius of Tyana*, 1.13, translation from Cartlidge and Dungan, *Documents for the Study of the Gospels*, 212.

by a wife, as were "the other apostles, and the brothers of the Lord, and Peter" (1 Cor. 9:5). Absent from both the accounts of Jesus and the letters of Paul is the attitude that sexual passion and reproduction are inherently unholy. The evidence suggests that this idea came to Christianity from Greek and Roman culture, not from the Jewish founders of Christianity.[27]

Gnosticism was very diverse and probably included a range of views on marriage. Some gnostic writings described marriage as a symbol of the divine union between male and female aspects or emanations of God,[28] but gnostics generally esteemed celibacy. It is possible that some gnostics used sexual intercourse as a ritual, as anti-gnostic critics sometimes charged, but gnostic writings available to us consistently promoted asceticism.[29] In these books, sexual reproduction was usually viewed negatively because it perpetuates the entrapment of souls in physical bodies when babies are born.[30] According to the gnostics, Christ came to tell us that we are heavenly beings trapped in this evil world that was created by an evil god, the god mistakenly worshipped by the Jews. Whether gnostic or not, in varying degrees and with varying justifications, the idea that physical passions and bodies are bad pervaded the literature of the second and third centuries of Christianity. This trend, and the accompanying trend toward anti-Semitism, became part of Christianity as it developed into a Roman religion and eventually became the official religion of the empire.

THE TEACHING OF THE TWELVE APOSTLES (DIDACHE)

An ancient document that provides a very early glimpse of Christianity is the Didache, or Teaching of the Twelve Apostles, probably dating from the late first century CE (based in part on its description of church organization). It may be older than some of the writings in the New Testament, and some historians date it, or portions of it, earlier than the Gospels of Matthew and Luke.[31] The Didache, which does not identify its author, was

---

27. For a thorough discussion of this topic see Pagels, *Adam, Eve, and the Serpent.*

28. *Gospel of Philip*, II, 3.70.10–23, in Robinson, *Nag Hammadi Library*, 151; see also Meyer, *Gospels of Mary.*

29. Ehrman, *Lost Christianities*, 126, 197–202.

30. For example, *The Testimony of Truth*, IX, 3.30, in Robinson, *Nag Hammadi Library*, 450.

31. Pagels, *Beyond Belief*, 15–18; Ehrman, *New Testament*, 447–50; Koester, *Ancient Christian Gospels*, 16–17; Harris, *New Testament*, ch. 20

mentioned by some church fathers as authoritative scripture, but it was lost until a copy was discovered in 1873 in a monastery in Constantinople. The Didache reveals a community rooted in Jewish traditions, but with a separate Christian identity. For example, the Didache says that "the hypocrites" (non-Christian Jews?) fast on Monday and Thursday, but "you should fast on Wednesday and Friday," to be distinct from them (Didache 8:1). This passage is reminiscent of Jesus' parable of the self-righteous Pharisee, who boasted that he "fasts twice in the week" (Luke 18:12). Instructions are given for baptism, which should be in cold, running water if available. If no water is available for immersion, water can be poured over the head three times, "in the name of the Father, Son and Holy Spirit" (cf. Matt. 28:19) Part of the Didache consists of instructions for daily life in the church, such as how to deal with itinerant prophets and teachers: If a prophet asks for money or orders a meal while prophesying in the Spirit, he is a false prophet; if he stays more than two days (!) he is a false prophet, unless he settles down with you. There are instructions for appointing leaders, and conducting the Eucharist (literally "thanksgiving") meal (Didache 9). There is no sign of the connection of the Eucharist with the body and blood of Lord as in the New Testament (Mark 14:22–25, 1 Cor. 11:23). The ritual words are different, and the order of bread and cup is reversed, with the cup first. Only people who have been baptized in the name of the Lord may partake of the Eucharist. There is a version of the Lord's Prayer, which should be prayed three times daily. These instructions provide insights into life and practice in this early Christian community, with some things familiar to modern Christians, and others strange.

Much of the Didache consists of ethical and doctrinal teachings that echo the synoptic Gospels, such as the command to love those who hate you, and a version of the Golden Rule. These sayings and the version of the Lord's Prayer are different enough from the four Gospels that they are not direct quotes, raising the tantalizing possibility that the Didache may represent an independent path of transmission for some of the sayings of Jesus. If these passages were dependent on one or more of the synoptic Gospels, then why was there no mention of the body and blood of the Lord in the description of the Eucharist, and why were the order and words of the Eucharist and the Lord's Prayer different from the Gospel accounts? The arrangement of the sayings also is different from the synoptic Gospels, grouping them in terms of two ways, the way of life and the way of death. For example, the Didache begins as follows:

There are two paths, one of life and one of death, and the difference between the two paths is great. This then is the path of life.
First, love the God who made you, and second, your neighbor as
yourself. And whatever you do not want to happen to you, do not
do to another.

This is the teaching related to this matter: Bless those who
curse you, pray for your enemies, and fast for those who persecute
you . . . You should love those who hate you, then you will have no
enemy. (Didache 1:1–3)

Concern for the poor is also expressed in the Didache, including the idea of
sharing things in common:

Do not shun a person in need, but share all things with your
brother and do not say that anything is your own. (Didache 4:8)[32]

Whether dependent on the synoptic Gospels or not, alternate versions
of familiar teachings of Jesus such as those in the Didache demonstrate
how some Christians understood and used these sayings, and how they
may have been transmitted before the Gospels we know were in use.[33] The
Didache closes with a statement of apocalyptic expectation similar to those
found in the New Testament, demonstrating that these Christians had the
same tradition:

Watch for your life's sake. Let not your lamps be quenched, nor
your clothes unfastened; but be ready, for you know not the hour
in which our Lord will come. For in the last days false prophets
and corrupters shall be multiplied, and the sheep shall be turned
into wolves, and love shall be turned into hate; for when lawless-
ness increases, they shall hate and persecute and betray one another, and then shall appear the world-deceiver as Son of God,
and shall do signs and wonders, and the earth shall be delivered
into his hands, and he shall do iniquitous things which have never
yet come to pass since the beginning. Then shall the creation of
men come into the fire of trial, and many shall be made to stumble
and shall perish; but those who endure in their faith shall be saved
from under the curse itself. And then shall appear the signs of the
truth: first, the sign of an outspreading in heaven, then the sign
of the sound of the trumpet. And third, the resurrection of the
dead—yet not of all, but as it is said: "The Lord shall come and all

---

32. Didache translated by Ehrman, *Lost Scriptures*, 212.

33. Pagels, *Beyond Belief*, 15–18.

His saints with Him." Then shall the world see the Lord coming upon the clouds of heaven. (Didache 16)[34]

These closing verses of the Didache contain many of the elements familiar from the apocalyptic prophecies and sayings found in the Gospels (see chapter 6). These include the admonition to be ready for the end to come suddenly, but also to watch for the signs, which include a false Son of God (as mentioned by Paul in 2 Thess. 2:3–12), and a time of great tribulation. The Didache and some other early Christian writings outside of the Bible provide valuable insights into the beginning of Christianity as a religion separate from Judaism, and contain alternate and possibly independent versions of some sayings of Jesus, but provide no new historical information about Jesus or his disciples.

THE NEW TESTAMENT CANON

Like many other early Christian writings both in and out of the Bible, the Didache was anonymous or if the authors were known this information has been lost. The hard truth is that by the late second century CE when the four Gospels and other early Christian writings were being circulated, no one knew who wrote them or how authentic they were, except for those written by the apostle Paul. Even Paul's writings were in dispute, because there were various books that claimed to have been written by prominent apostles and it was clear some were fakes. The New Testament writings were preserved, while other writings were not, based on a judgment by influential church leaders that these were the oldest and most authentic Christian writings. This judgment was based in part on tradition and in part on what these leaders thought the gospel ought to say.[35]

After the Roman Emperor Constantine ended the persecution of Christians and began official support for Christianity in 313 CE (see chapter 11), church leaders became more powerful, and bishops such as those in Rome and Alexandria attempted to bring conformity to Christianity. The church historian Eusebius of Caesarea, writing in the early fourth century, described twenty-one books of the New Testament as widely accepted,

---

34. Didache translated by Robert Donaldson, from Kirby, *Early Christian Writings.* See also Ehrman, *Lost Scriptures*, 217.

35. See Ehrman, *Lost Christianities*, on the diversity of writings and development of the canon; also Ehrman, *Misquoting Jesus*, ch. 1; Harris, *New Testament*, ch. 1, 20.

with others in dispute.[36] Six disputed books that were eventually included in the New Testament were: James, Jude, 2 Peter, 2 and 3 John, and Revelation (Apocalypse of John). Other candidates that did not make the final cut were the Acts of Paul and Thecla, Shepherd of Hermas, Apocalypse of Peter, Epistle of Barnabas, and the Didache. Eusebius rejected other books, including the Gospel of Thomas, saying their style was not apostolic and their content was heretical.

In 367 CE, Athanasius the Bishop of Alexandria included in his Easter letter to Egyptian churches a list of books officially approved as divinely inspired scripture. This is the earliest known canonical list to conform to the one Christians use today.[37] In this letter, Athanasius urged all Christians under his supervision to cleanse the church of other Christian writings, because, he said, they are defiled and filled with myths. It may have been at this time that monks at a monastery near the town of Nag Hammadi took the precaution of gathering more than fifty books from their library and burying them in a pottery jar where they were found 1600 years later. These included the Gospel of Thomas and other lost books. Eventually the canon cited by Athanasius came to be the one accepted by almost all Christians, as it was adopted by the powerful Roman church.

It turns out that the four Gospels of the New Testament are, in fact, the best sources we have for the life and teaching of Jesus. Four Gospels were preserved in the Christian Bible, rather than one or a synthesis of the four, because Christian leaders could not agree on a single or unified version and thought all four were valuable.[38] Earlier sources used by the authors of these four Gospels are now lost. Many other early writings that would have been useful for historians of Christianity, such as the Gospel of Peter, the Gospel of the Nazareans, and other non-canonical gospels are lost or available only in fragments—in part because Christian scribes in later centuries did not consider them worth copying or were forbidden to use them. For some early Christian writings, the only surviving sources are in the writings of church "fathers" such as Eusebius and Irenaeus (c.180 CE) who quoted them in the context of criticizing them.[39] This was the main source

---

36. Eusebius, *Ecclesiastical History*, 3.25.1–7; Harris, *New Testament*, 11.

37. For this and other versions of the New Testament canon see Ehrman, *Lost Scriptures*, 330–342.

38. Ehrman, *Jesus: Apocalyptic Prophet*, 43. Harris, *New Testament*, 12.

39. See Ehrman, *Lost Scriptures*, for reconstructions of some early documents from excerpts in the writings of Eusebius and other sources.

of information about gnostic Christians before the discovery in 1945 of the library buried at Nag Hammadi. The writings found there, and similar recent discoveries such as the gospels of Mary and Judas,[40] reveal much about the diversity of Christianity but little about the historical Jesus, despite sensational claims of books like *The Da Vinci Code*. The four Gospels are the best evidence available for who Jesus was and what he did, but other writings help to build the context essential to understand what the Gospels intended to communicate and their place in history.

---

40. Pagels and King, *Reading Judas*

8

Josephus and the New Testament

JESUS AND HIS BROTHER JAMES

The books of the Bible came from a culture and a time, as any writings do, so it makes sense to look for other writings from the broader Jewish and Roman world that might shed light on the lives of Jesus and his followers. Unfortunately, there is very little to work with despite the existence of a large number of documents from the Roman Empire in the time of Jesus.[1] As a Jewish peasant who was executed by the Romans, Jesus did not get much notice until Christianity began to spread. To most people, Christianity looked like just another Jewish sect until it gained a following among non-Jews and they transformed it into a Roman religion.

Jewish rabbis passed on stories of important Jewish teachers and leaders such as Hillel, a contemporary of Jesus previously mentioned for his use of the Golden Rule. These stories give some insight into the thinking of some Jews at the time of Jesus, but were filtered through centuries of editing before reaching their modern form in the Mishnah and Talmud in the fifth and sixth centuries CE.[2] Philo of Alexandria (the Jewish/Roman philosopher and contemporary of Jesus) provided the perspective of a Jew who also thought of himself as a Roman, attempting the bridge the gap between the two worlds in his writings. He supplied some useful historical details

---

1. Ehrman, *Jesus: Apocalyptic Prophet*, ch. 4; Levine et al., *Historical Jesus*; Cartlidge and Dungan, *Documents for the Study of the Gospels*.

2. Levine, *Misunderstood Jew*, ch.1; A.J. Avery-Peck, "The Galilean charismatic and rabbinic piety: the holy man in Talmudic literature," ch. 8 in Levine et al., *Historical Jesus*; Schiffman, *Understanding Second Temple and Rabbinic Judaism*.

such as descriptions of the Essenes and the rule of Pilate.[3] The Dead Sea Scrolls provide a detailed look into the lives and teachings of the religious community at Qumran that produced the scrolls. This library shows that Jesus, John the Baptist, and their disciples were part of a wider culture of Jews critical of the temple priesthood in Jerusalem, and who expected the imminent coming of a Messiah to bring the Kingdom of God.[4]

The most important historical source apart from the Bible for understanding first-century Judaism is the work of Flavius Josephus, the Jewish historian and apologist born in 37 CE in Galilee, the home of Jesus. Josephus was mentioned previously for his descriptions of Essenes, apocalyptic prophets, and the fall of Jerusalem. Without Josephus we would know very little about Jewish culture or events from the time of Jesus, or the Jewish-Roman war that happened at the same time that Christianity was growing and spreading. His vast works on the history and culture of the Jewish people provide a wealth of information available nowhere else.[5] For example, Josephus' descriptions of the Pharisees and Sadducees supply almost all of the information known about these important Jewish sects outside of the New Testament. His accounts of uprisings and rebel leaders, some mentioned in the New Testament such as Theudas and "the Egyptian" (Acts 5:36, 21:38), are invaluable for understanding the politically charged atmosphere in which Jesus lived. These included a revolt not long after Jesus was born when thousands of rebels were crucified in Jerusalem, and a tax revolt led by Judas the Galilean while Jesus was a young boy (about 6 CE) that also ended in bloody violence (see Acts 5:37). Josephus described in detail the reign of Herod the Great and his vast building programs, including the fabulous Jerusalem Temple that was one of the wonders of the ancient world. He explained how this temple functioned in the lives of the Jews, as at Passover when many thousands of people gathered for the annual rituals. He described a state-of-the-art Roman port at Caesarea Maritima built by Herod the Great and dedicated to Emperor Caesar Augustus, and the development of the Galilean cities of Sepphoris and Tiberias by Herod's son Antipas. Tiberias was a new capital of the Galilee province, dedicated to Emperor Tiberias. These accounts have been supported by recent archaeo-

---

3. G.E. Sterling, "Philo of Alexandria," ch. 18 in Levine et al., *Historical Jesus*.

4. Schiffman, *Qumran and Jerusalem*.

5. See Crossan and Reed, *Excavating Jesus*; Goldberg, *Flavius Josephus Home Page*; Ehrman, *Jesus: Apocalyptic Prophet*; C. Evans, "Josephus on John the Baptist and other Jewish prophets," ch. 2 in Levine et al., *Historical Jesus*.

logical discoveries.[6] According to Josephus, these cities were resented by Galilean Jews as symbols of corrupt rule under Rome. Sepphoris, only four miles from Jesus' home town of Nazareth, was modernized and expanded under Herod Antipas while Jesus was growing up nearby.

Josephus mentioned Jesus only twice in passing. The longest reference is disappointingly short, only a few sentences within a longer passage about Pilate, reporting that Jesus was a wise and popular teacher who was executed by Pilate but still had some followers after his death.[7] The passage as it exists today says some clearly Christian things such as "he was the Christ [Messiah]." Josephus would not have said this because he was not a Christian, demonstrating that his words were edited. He may actually have written something like "he was *called* the Christ," since Jesus was known as "Jesus the Christ." This paragraph must have been changed to make a Christian statement by the scribes who passed it on, obscuring Josephus' actual words for all time. Christians copied and preserved the writings of Josephus, while Jews generally considered him a traitor for his cooperation with the Romans after he surrendered during the war.

If Josephus really thought Jesus was the Messiah he would have given him more than a few sentences. John the Baptist and Pilate are much more prominent in his accounts than Jesus. However, Josephus provides historical corroboration and a different perspective for the lives of Jesus, John the Baptist, Pilate, High Priest Caiaphas, and Herod the Great and his sons, and shows that John the Baptist was popular and well-known in his time. His description of Pilate as unpopular, provocative, and brutal was corroborated by Philo of Alexandria,[8] and shows that Pilate would not have hesitated to execute anyone deemed a troublemaker or subversive. Even Pilate's Roman superiors considered him unnecessarily brutal and he was recalled in 37 CE after a particularly bloody massacre of Samaritans, again a case of a prophet who gathered a following and ended in disaster at the hands of the Romans.[9] Josephus was writing in Rome about 90 CE, so he may have heard about Jesus as a young man in Galilee, or as an older Jewish historian in Rome where Christians or Jews could have told him the story.

---

6. Crossan and Reed, *Excavating Jesus*.

7. Josephus, *Antiquities* 18.3.3.

8. Philo of Alexandria, "On The Embassy of Gaius," 299–305, translation by G.E. Sterling, 303–304 in Levine et al., *Historical Jesus*.

9. Josephus, *Antiquities* 18.4.2.

Here is his description of Jesus, with brackets and italics to indicate phrases that were probably inserted later, and the word "called" added:

> At this time there appeared Jesus, a wise man [*if indeed one should call him a man*]. For he was a doer of startling deeds, a teacher of people who receive the truth with pleasure. And he gained a following both among many Jews and among many of Greek origin. He was [called] the Christ. And when Pilate [*, because of an accusation made by the leading men among us,*][10] condemned him to the cross, those who had loved him previously did not cease to do so. [*For he appeared to them on the third day, living again, just as the divine prophets had spoken of these and countless other wondrous things about him.*] And up until this very day the tribe of Christians, named after him, has not died out.[11]

Saying that Jesus was "called" the Christ would identify Jesus for his Roman readers as "Jesus the Christ" of the Christians. This is consistent with Josephus' only other reference to Jesus, an account of the execution by stoning of James and some companions at the instigation of the High Priest Ananus about 62 CE. Josephus noted that James, "brother of Jesus who is called the Christ," was respected by those who were "strict in observance of the law," and they objected to the execution of James.[12] His account portrayed James and his associates continuing to live in Jerusalem as observant Jews who were Christians. They had the respect of other observant Jews who were probably Pharisees, but hostility from the priests and Sadducees who also had supported the execution of James' older brother Jesus.

High Priest Ananus took advantage of a break in the Roman succession of officials to kill James, when the Roman procurator died in office and his replacement had not yet arrived. This is reminiscent of the account of the trial of Jesus in John (18:31), when the High Priest Caiaphas told Pilate that his Jewish court was not allowed to put a man to death so the Romans would have to do it. Ananus acted on his own to kill Jesus' brother James, but later had to account for this to the new Roman procurator Albinus. Jews who were sympathetic to James complained to Albinus and he replaced Ananus as High Priest because of these complaints. This account confirms the presence

---

10. This phrase about "the leading men among us" may have been added, as it is uncharacteristically vague about which Jews were intended, and may reflect the tendency of later Christians to blame Jews and exonerate Pilate.

11. Josephus, *Antiquities*, 18.3.3, translation based on Ehrman, *New Testament*, 214.

12. Josephus, *Antiquities*, 20.9.1; for discussion see Crossan and Reed, *Excavating Jesus*, ch. 1.

of Jesus' brother James in Jerusalem, explains what happened to this important Jewish Christian leader, confirms the Roman control over the Jewish High Priest, and helps to set the stage in which the events played out.

This account of James living in Jerusalem as an observant Jew is consistent with the New Testament. The four Gospels describe Jesus' family as unsupportive of his mission (Mark 3:21, 31–35; John 7:5), but either this was exaggerated or at some point it changed. His mother Mary was among the women who went with Jesus to Jerusalem from Galilee for the Passover, for she is said to have been present at his death (John 19:25), and the Acts of the Apostles placed Mary and the brothers of Jesus with the other leading disciples in Jerusalem after the resurrection of Jesus (Acts 1:14). Though the Gospels did not relate the story of James seeing the risen Jesus, Paul passed on the information that James was an important witness (1 Cor. 15:7). In the Acts of the Apostles, Peter and John were mentioned as prominent leaders along with James. He was a leader of Jewish Christians who were strict in observance of the Jewish laws (Acts 15:13, 21:18). This was confirmed by Paul, who described a conflict he had with some people "from James" who wanted his non-Jewish converts to follow Jewish practices of circumcision and dietary restrictions (see chapter 9). These references from the New Testament fit well with the description of James provided by Josephus. James was a Christian leader, but he saw this as entirely consistent with his Jewishness, and continued to live in Jerusalem and follow the Jewish laws. The respect given James by other observant Jews is consistent with passages in the Acts of the Apostles about Pharisees who were Christian believers (Acts 15:5), and a prominent Pharisee named Gamaliel who interceded for Christian leaders when they were arrested and beaten by the High Priest and the Sadducees (Acts 5:34–39).

JOHN THE BAPTIST AND THE MESSIAH

One thing that comes through in all four Gospels is a strong link between John the Baptist and Jesus, and some of John's disciples became disciples of Jesus (John 1:35–37, 3:22–30; Acts 1:5, 18:24–26). After the death of John, some people even said that Jesus was John risen from the dead (Mark 6:14, 8:28). John and Jesus had a similar message: Repent, to escape the coming judgment; in the meantime, share with those who have less, and avoid violence (Luke 3:10–14). John preached righteousness and foretold a Messiah coming soon to judge the earth (Mark 1:7–8). Later, Christians said John had been right and Jesus was the Messiah he had predicted.

Josephus wrote an extensive account of John the Baptist, with parallels to the Gospel reports of his execution by Herod Antipas, son of Herod the Great (Mark 6:14–29, Matt. 14:1–13). According to Josephus it was the fact that John gathered a large following that resulted in his death:

> For Herod [Antipas] had him killed, although he was a good man and had urged the Jews to exert themselves to virtue, both as to justice toward one another and reverence towards God, and having done so join together in baptism. For immersion in water, it was clear to him, could not be used for the forgiveness of sins, but to sanctify the body, and only if the soul was already thoroughly purified by right actions. And when others massed about him, for they were very greatly moved by his words, Herod, who feared that such strong influence over the people might carry to a revolt—for they seemed ready to do anything he should advise—believed it much better to move now than later have it raise a rebellion and engage him in actions he would regret.[13]

Jews had various rituals that involved bathing as part of ritual purification, and the Dead Sea Scrolls describe some of these,[14] but John added his own meaning to baptism as a sign of repentance and devotion to God. The synoptic Gospels describe John the Baptist as wearing a rough garment of camel hair, with a leather belt, and living on locusts and wild honey (Mark 1:6). This is reminiscent of the description of the famous prophet Elijah in the Old Testament (2 Kings 1:8), but Josephus provided another interesting parallel, in his description of Jewish sects:

> When I was about sixteen years old I had a mind to make a trial of the several sects that were among us. There are three of these, that of the Pharisees, the Sadducees, and the third that of the Essenes. I thought that being acquainted with them all I could choose the best.
>
> So I consigned myself to hardship, and underwent great difficulties, and went through them all. Nor did I content myself with the trying of these three only, for when I was informed that one whose name was Banus lived in the desert, and used no other clothing than what grew upon trees, and had no other food than what grew of its own accord, and bathed himself in cold water

---

13. Josephus, *Antiquities*, 18.5.2, translation based on Whiston, *Josephus*.

14. P. Flint, "Jesus and the Dead Sea Scrolls," 110–31 in Levine et al., *Historical Jesus*.

> frequently, both night and day, to purify himself, I imitated him in
> those things, and continued with him three years.[15]

Three years in the desert living on whatever grew on its own, such as locusts and wild honey! Josephus seems to place this Banus in a category by himself, a religious ascetic with remarkable parallels to John the Baptist as described in the Gospels. Josephus was an earnestly religious young man growing up in Galilee, the home of Jesus. It is easy to imagine John the Baptist or Jesus in Josephus' place, exploring the various schools of thought available to them, fasting and praying in the desert.

The description of John the Baptist by Josephus includes the familiar call to justice and virtue, with baptism as a sign of this commitment, but conspicuously absent is John's apocalyptic, messianic message as in the Gospel accounts. This aspect of Jewish thought and belief is also missing from Josephus' accounts of the Pharisees, Essenes, and others. It is clear from other sources and even Josephus that the messianic expectation was strong at the time among Jews in Palestine, so why was it downplayed in his writings? To understand this, it is necessary to understand the purpose of Josephus in writing his histories of the Jewish-Roman war (*The Jewish War*) and of the Jewish people (*Antiquities of the Jews*).

After surrendering in the lost war of 66–70 CE, Josephus took the attitude "if you can't beat them, join them." According to his own account, when the uprising against Rome broke out in 66 CE he was against war, but he ended up at the age of about thirty in command of all the troops in Galilee, and gave it a valiant effort. Much of his energy was expended dealing with infighting among the Jewish factions, but he was involved in some major battles with the Romans. In the end, all was lost, and he found himself hiding in a cave with about forty other Jewish fighters. The Romans found them and offered him (the leading officer) an opportunity to surrender and possibly save his life, to which he agreed, but his fellow soldiers would not allow it and threatened to kill him. Probably they expected they would be crucified. In the end they made a suicide pack by drawing lots for who would be killed next, but somehow after about thirty-nine assisted suicides it came down to just Josephus and one other, whom he persuaded to join him in surrendering. Josephus said he had prophetic dreams that had told him the Romans would conquer so he knew the war was lost before it started.[16]

---

15. Josephus, *Life*, 2.10, translation from Goldberg, "New Testament Parallels," in *Flavius Josephus Home Page*.

16. Josephus, *War*, 2.8.2

When Josephus met the Roman general Vespasian and his son Titus, Josephus told Vespasian that he, Josephus, was a prophet and that Vespasian would be the next Emperor of Rome. Vespasian thought Josephus was just flattering him at first, but kept him around and treated him well. Josephus served as a translator and negotiator during the final siege of Jerusalem. His prophecy about Vespasian was soon fulfilled when the Emperor Nero killed himself in 68 CE and Vespasian became Emperor and left for Rome. Josephus continued serving Vespasian's son Titus, who took over to finish the bloody siege of Jerusalem. After the war ended, Josephus was freed and adopted into Vespasian's family, a relationship that continued when Titus succeeded his father as Emperor. Josephus took the name Flavius, became a Roman citizen, and was given an apartment in Rome and a commission to write the official history of the war.[17]

Josephus in his writings expressed gratitude to Vespasian and Titus, his patrons. He took on the task of explaining Jewish history and culture to the Romans, who might view Jews as troublemakers who got what they deserved, with strange customs that did not make sense. In this context, Josephus was very careful in what he said about the messianic expectation of the Jews, which after all was a challenge to the authority of Rome. Josephus acknowledged that the coming Messiah was a commonly held belief, but blamed militaristic zealots for exploiting this hope and bringing on the disastrous war.[18] He described Jerusalem with its charged atmosphere of inflamed expectations as "a place doomed to destruction" even before the Romans attacked.[19] To explain the war to his Roman audience, Josephus said the Jews misunderstood their own prophecies:

> But what more than all else incited them to the war was an ambiguous oracle also found in their sacred writings, that: "At about that time, one from their country would become ruler of the habitable world."
>
> This they took to mean one of their own people, and many of the wise men were misled in their interpretation. This oracle, however, in reality signified the government of Vespasian, who was proclaimed Emperor while in Judea.[20]

---

17. Josephus, *Life*, 76.

18. Josephus, *War*, 4.6.3.

19. Ibid., 2.22.1

20. Ibid., 6.6.4, translation from Goldberg, "New Testament Parallels," in *Flavius Josephus Home Page*; see also Crossan and Reed, *Excavating Jesus*, ch. 5.

In this amazing passage, Josephus summed up his public opinion of the messianic hope of the Jews: it was all a tragic misunderstanding. The prophecy was really about the Roman Emperor Vespasian, he was the Messiah everyone hoped for! It is not clear how much of this Josephus actually believed, but this explains why Josephus did not mention the messianic views of Pharisees, Essenes, John the Baptist, Jesus, or anyone he presented in a sympathetic light for his Roman audience—he did not want to tarnish them as promoters of the mistaken messianic expectation, which he said was the cause of the war. He said Jesus was called "the Christ" but never explained to his Roman readers what this meant. He blamed the war on zealots who deceived people and exploited their hope, and he removed the apocalyptic, messianic element from the rest of the discussion.[21]

The oracle referred to by Josephus seems to be based on Deuteronomy 18:15–19, in which Moses promised that God will raise up another prophet like Moses, with God's words in his mouth. This was one of the foundational passages of messianic Judaism, cited not only by Josephus, but also Philo of Alexandria,[22] and in the New Testament with reference to Jesus (Acts 7:37). Another important passage that points to the Messiah is from the prophet Malachi:

> Behold I send my messenger to prepare the way . . . but who can endure the day of his coming, and who can stand when he appears? (Mal. 3:1, 2).

> For behold, the day comes, burning like an oven, when all the arrogant and all evildoers will be stubble; the day that comes shall burn them up, says the Lord of hosts, so that it will leave them neither root nor branch. But for you who fear my name the sun of righteousness shall rise, with healing in its wings. You shall go forth leaping like calves from the stall. And you shall tread down the wicked, for they will be ashes under the soles of your feet, on the day when I act, says the Lord of hosts. Remember the law of my servant Moses, the statutes and ordinances that I commanded him at Horeb for all Israel. Behold, I will send you Elijah the prophet before the great and terrible day of the Lord comes. And he will turn the hearts of fathers to their children and the hearts of children to their fathers, lest I come and smite the land with a curse. (Mal. 4, RSV)

---

21. C.A. Evans, "Josephus on John the Baptist and other Jewish prophets," 55–63 in Levine et al., *Historical Jesus*.

22. Philo, *On Rewards and Punishments*, 95.

This prophecy in Malachi was reflected in a belief among some apocalyptic Jews that the great prophet Elijah would return to prepare the way for the Messiah. According to the synoptic Gospels, some people thought Jesus might be the return of the prophet Elijah (Mark 6:14–15, 8:28). Some early Christians believed John the Baptist was this forerunner of the Messiah, and they applied these prophecies to him (Matt. 11:7–15), though in the Gospel of John he was quoted denying that he was Elijah or "that prophet" (John 1:20–22). Apparently, this idea of the forerunner prophet Elijah was a common part of the messianic expectation, as it shows up in different versions in these Gospels. Josephus did not share the messianic beliefs of some of his contemporaries such as the followers of Jesus, but he understood the importance of these beliefs to his fellow Jews in the events leading up to the war and the destruction of Jerusalem.

9

Paul, Peter, James, and the Gospel

THE GOSPEL ACCORDING TO PAUL

The Gospels contain sayings and stories that originated with Jesus and were later written down, but the oldest writings in the New Testament are the letters of Paul. Allowing for a few years after the death of Jesus when Paul was persecuting Christians before his conversion (Gal. 1:13, Acts 8:1–3), and fourteen years as he began his work according to his account (Gal. 1:18, 2:1), this puts his letters in the 50s CE. This dating is confirmed by his hearing before Felix who was the procurator of Judea in 52–58 CE (Acts 24:27). Paul did not know the earthly Jesus, and made a new version of Christianity with his message to non-Jews.

Paul, by his own account (Phil. 3:5, Acts 23:6), was a Pharisee. The Pharisees were described by Josephus as strict in following the Jewish laws,[1] and like Jesus and his disciples they believed in the future resurrection of the dead (Acts 23:6–8). Paul agreed with the persecution of Jesus and his followers, and tried to stamp out the new Jewish sect of Christians. In his letter to the Galatians, Paul described how he was converted to following Jesus through a revelation, and argued on this basis that he had a right to speak independently of the Christian leaders in Jerusalem:

> For I would have you know, brethren, that the gospel which was preached by me is not man's gospel. For I did not receive it from man, nor was I taught it, but it came through a revelation of Jesus Christ. For you have heard of my former life in Judaism, how I persecuted the church of God violently and tried to destroy it; and

---

1. Josephus, *Antiquities*, 18.1.2–3; *War*, 2.8.14.

I advanced in Judaism beyond many of my own age among my people, so extremely zealous was I for the traditions of my fathers. But when he who had set me apart before I was born, and had called me through his grace, was pleased to reveal his Son to me, in order that I might preach him among the Gentiles, I did not confer with flesh and blood, nor did I go up to Jerusalem to those who were apostles before me, but I went away into Arabia; and again I returned to Damascus. Then after three years I went up to Jerusalem to visit Cephas [Peter], and remained with him fifteen days. But I saw none of the other apostles except James the Lord's brother. (In what I am writing to you, before God, I do not lie!) Then I went into the regions of Syria and Cilicia. And I was still not known by sight to the churches of Christ in Judea; they only heard it said, "He who once persecuted us is now preaching the faith he once tried to destroy." (Gal. 1:11–23, RSV)

In this passage Paul emphasized his independence because he was writing to criticize the Christian leaders. Paul was aware he was on shaky ground since he had not been a follower of Jesus and in fact had persecuted them. Although he said he did not confer with these leaders right away, he would have met with other Christians, as described in the Acts of the Apostles (Acts 9, 22). Paul's conversion was a turning point in history, as his mission to non-Jews probably was responsible for the fact that Christianity survived and spread even after the destruction of Jerusalem. Paul did not describe his conversion in detail in his letters, but it was described in the Acts of the Apostles, which may have been written by a traveling companion of Paul. He certainly would have told this story, as it was the basis for his claim to be an apostle and a witness of the risen Jesus (1 Cor. 15:8–9), so it is possible that the author of the book heard it as told by Paul. At the time of his conversion Paul went by "Saul," a Jewish name, rather than "Paul," a Roman name:

But Saul, still breathing threats and murder against the disciples of the Lord, went to the high priest and asked him for letters to the synagogues at Damascus, so that if he found any belonging to the Way, men or women, he might bring them bound to Jerusalem. Now as he journeyed he approached Damascus, and suddenly a light from heaven flashed about him. And he fell to the ground and heard a voice saying to him, "Saul, Saul, why do you persecute me?" And he said, "Who are you, Lord?" And he said, "I am Jesus, whom you are persecuting; but rise and enter the city, and you will be told what you are to do."

> The men who were traveling with him stood speechless, hearing the voice but seeing no one. Saul arose from the ground; and when his eyes were opened, he could see nothing; so they led him by the hand and brought him into Damascus. And for three days he was without sight, and neither ate nor drank. (Acts 9:1–9, RSV; see also Acts 22)

In Damascus, Paul met some Christians who helped him and he began preaching that Jesus really was the Christ, the Son of God. Thus began the missionary work of Paul that eventually transformed the Roman Empire and the world, and produced letters that today compose much of the New Testament.

Though the Gospels were composed after the letters of Paul, they do not appear to use Paul as a source, and draw on earlier sources about the actions and teachings of Jesus. Some of these early oral traditions were known to Paul. When he related the story of the Last Supper (1 Cor. 11:23–25), and the resurrection of Jesus (1 Cor. 15:3–8), he said he was relaying these things as he heard them from other Christians. When he quoted the teaching of Jesus on divorce, Paul was careful to point out that it was not him but "the Lord" who said it (1 Cor. 7:10, 12, 25). In what was probably his earliest letter, 1 Thessalonians, Paul attributed the apocalyptic message to Jesus:

> For since we believe that Jesus died and rose again, even so, through Jesus, God will bring with him those who have fallen asleep. For this we declare to you *by the word of the Lord*, that we who are alive, who are left until the coming of the Lord, shall not precede those who have fallen asleep. For the Lord himself will descend from heaven with a cry of command, with the archangel's call, and with the sound of the trumpet of God. And the dead in Christ will rise first; then we who are alive, who are left, shall be caught up together with them in the clouds to meet the Lord in the air; and so we shall always be with the Lord. (1 Thess. 4:11–17, RSV, emphasis added)

Earlier in this same letter, Paul summarized his message to non-Jews as follows:

> You turned to God from idols, to serve a living and true God, and to wait for his Son from heaven, whom he raised from the dead, Jesus who delivers us from the wrath to come. (1 Thess. 1:9–10, RSV)

The "wrath to come" referred to the judgment that will come on the Day of the Lord. It is unclear how much of the details of his message Paul attributed to Jesus, but there is no evidence that he was in disagreement with the Gospels or the disciples of Jesus about the basic Christian message.

Paul in his letters said little of the teachings of Jesus, probably because the stories and sayings of Jesus were passed from others and so did not provide the basis for independent authority that Paul claimed. He was more concerned with his own message *about* Jesus, based on personal revelation from the spirit of the resurrected Jesus. Thus, Paul embodied a tension between personal revelation and centralized authority in Christianity that continued through the writings of the gnostics and up to the present day.

PAUL, PETER, AND JAMES

Though they agreed on much of the basic message, Paul was not in complete agreement with the Jerusalem church led by Peter and James (the brother of Jesus). The argument was about whether gentiles (non-Jews) could become Christians without adopting the Jewish laws; and it was about whether Jews should relax their observance of these laws to fellowship with gentile Christians.[2] Particularly striking is a passage in the letter to the Galatians, in which Paul described a confrontation with Peter and some people "sent from James." Paul began by describing a meeting with James, Peter (Cephas) and John (son of Zebedee), the leaders of the Jerusalem Christians:

> . . . James and Cephas and John, who were reputed to be pillars [leaders], gave to me and Barnabas the right hand of fellowship, that we should go to the Gentiles and they to the circumcised [Jews]; only they would have us remember the poor, which very thing I was eager to do. But when Cephas came to Antioch I opposed him to his face, because he stood condemned. For before certain men came from James, he ate with the Gentiles; but when they came he drew back and separated himself, fearing the circumcision party. And with him the rest of the Jews acted insincerely, so that even Barnabas was carried away by their insincerity. But when I saw that they were not straightforward about the truth of the gospel, I said to Cephas before them all, "If you, though a Jew, live like a Gentile and not like a Jew, how can you compel the Gentiles to live like Jews? We ourselves, who are Jews by birth and not Gentile sinners, yet who know that a man is not justified by

2. See Levine, *Misunderstood Jew*, ch. 2; Crossan and Reed, *Excavating Jesus*, ch. 1,4.

works of the law but through faith in Jesus Christ, even we have believed in Christ Jesus, in order to be justified by faith in Christ, and not by works of the law, because by works of the law shall no one be justified." (Gal. 2:9–16, RSV)

Paul was upset that his non-Jewish converts, whom he did not require to convert to Judaism, were not being given equal fellowship with Jewish Christians. In this example the conflict was over dietary laws, but circumcision was perhaps even more important as a line of division. He described those from James as "the circumcision party" because they wanted gentile Christian converts to be converts to Judaism, who must be circumcised. As I now read this account from Paul "opposing Peter to his face" and telling him "he stood condemned," I imagine Peter struggling to compose himself, saying, "Paul, you didn't know Jesus, you weren't even there! With Jesus we always observed the Jewish laws, and he did not tell us to do otherwise. We gave you approval to convert gentiles, but now you want to tell us to stop following our own laws?"

Peter's position in this passage, caught in the middle between Paul and James, is also seen in the Acts of the Apostles where Peter is depicted as leading the Jerusalem church to be more open to gentiles, after he was guided to this by a vision. He preached to the house of Cornelius, a gentile who asked Peter to speak God's message to a gathering of Cornelius' relatives and friends. They believed his message and received the Holy Spirit, "speaking in tongues and extolling God." Peter baptized them and stayed with them several days (Acts 10:48), though it was against Jewish practice to eat with gentiles. He is quoted as telling them, "God has shown me that I should not call any man common or unclean" (Acts 10:28). Before this, preachers spreading the message of Jesus as the Christ, the Jewish Messiah, went only to Jews (Acts 11:18, Matt. 15:24). Word of this new development got back to Jerusalem and Peter was challenged to explain himself:

So when Peter went up to Jerusalem, the circumcision party criticized him, saying, "Why did you go to uncircumcised men and eat with them?" But Peter explained to them: "I was in the city of Joppa praying; and in a trance I saw a vision, something descending, like a great sheet, let down from heaven by four corners; and it came down to me. Looking at it closely I observed animals and beasts of prey and reptiles and birds of the air. And I heard a voice saying to me, 'Rise, Peter; kill and eat.' But I said, 'No, Lord; for nothing common or unclean has ever entered my mouth.' But the voice answered a second time from heaven, 'What God has cleansed you must not call common.' This happened three times, and all was drawn up again into heaven. At that very moment three men arrived at the house in which we were, sent to me from Caesarea. And the Spirit told me to go with them, making no distinction [between Jew or gentile]. These six brethren also accompanied me, and we entered the man's house. And he [Cornelius] told us how he had seen the angel standing in his house and saying, 'Send to Joppa and bring Simon called Peter; he will declare to you a message by which you will be saved, you and all your household.' As I began to speak, the Holy Spirit fell on them just as on us at the beginning [Acts 2:1–4]. And I remembered the word of the Lord, how he said, 'John baptized with water, but you shall be baptized with the Holy Spirit.' If then God gave the same gift to them as he gave to us when we believed in the Lord Jesus Christ, who was I that I could withstand God?" When they heard this they were silenced. And they glorified God, saying, "Then to the Gentiles also God has granted repentance unto life." (Acts 11:2–18, RSV)

If God has also granted life to gentiles, then they can have eternal life and enter the Kingdom of Heaven when Christ returns, the same as Jewish believers. There was no disagreement about the basic idea of the Kingdom of Heaven and the coming resurrection, just a question of whether or not it is open to non-Jews. In this version of the story the "circumcision party" was won over by Peter's explanation, but Paul's account in Galatians shows that not everyone was satisfied with this outcome and the reality was messier.

After a conference with Paul, James and the Jerusalem leaders issued a letter to Paul's gentile converts saying they did not have to keep the Jewish ritual laws of circumcision and diet (Acts 15:19–35). Given this letter of agreement, what was the continuing conflict about? There are clues in these two passages I have quoted: Peter's speech before the Jewish Christians and Paul's diatribe against Peter. Peter was willing to relax the Jewish dietary laws when necessary to reach out to gentiles, but this did not mean a general decision that Christians, especially Jewish Christians, would give up following the Jewish laws. When he went to Antioch in Galatia, he made an exception to fellowship with gentiles, as he had with the house of Cornelius; but when Jewish Christians who adhered to the laws arrived, he saw no contradiction in joining them for a kosher meal. Peter was doing something radical by reaching out to gentiles at all, but Paul condemned him as a hypocrite for joining Jewish Christians who followed the dietary laws as Peter and Jesus had always done. Paul was alone in this position, as even his partner Barnabus agreed with Peter. Some of these Jewish Christians also disagreed with Paul about the need for gentile converts to be circumcised, contradicting the letter from Jerusalem described in the book of Acts. This suggests that James and Peter were in a difficult position and many of their Jewish Christian associates did not agree with opening up Christian fellowship to gentiles unless they also became practicing Jews.

There were three cultural practices that clearly set Jews apart from the rest of the Roman world: circumcision of males, dietary laws, and observance of the Sabbath and other Jewish holy days.[3] The dominant Greek/Roman culture did not practice circumcision and many people thought the practice was backward and barbaric. Observant Jews refused to work on the Sabbath day; and Jews viewed gentile foods as "unclean" both in content and preparation, and would not eat with gentiles. If non-Jews had to adopt these Jewish practices to become Christians, this would set up major cultural barriers to their inclusion in the Christian community, and Paul did not want this. He argued that the sacrifice of Jesus made these practices unnecessary, and only faith in Jesus was needed for gentiles to be included in God's plan of salvation. They need only love one another to fulfill the requirements of the law (Rom. 13:8–10, Gal. 5:14). Although this principle had been stated by Jesus and other Jewish teachers (see chapter 4), Paul was pushing for taking it quite literally, challenging some of the central practices of the Jewish tradition.

For Peter, his willingness to baptize gentiles and join them in fellowship did not necessarily mean gentiles would be entirely exempt from Jewish practices, nor did it mean Jews should abandon their own adherence to what they believed were the laws of God. Peter could accept gentiles but still be a Jew himself as he had always been. These things still had to be worked out. Paul saw the conflict with other Jewish Christians as a barrier to his ministry, and emphasized that he got James and Peter to see it his way. The book of Acts was friendly to Paul's position and played down the conflict. We do not know what Peter, James and the other disciples said or thought, but reading between the lines, this issue apparently was not resolved as neatly as the author of Acts suggested.

As already discussed (chapter 8), according to Josephus, James died in 62 CE still living in Jerusalem and following the Jewish laws, with the

---

3. Levine, *Misunderstood Jew*; Ehrman, *New Testament*, 39; Levine and Brettler, *Jewish Annotated New Testament*, 514; Schiffman, *Understanding Second Temple and Rabbinic Judaism*, ch. 7.

respect of other Jews who were "strict in the observance of the laws."[4] Some Christian believers still identified with the Jewish sect of the Pharisees (Acts 15:5), demonstrating how much agreement existed between Pharisees and Christians about basic doctrine. A Pharisee could be a Christian simply by believing that Jesus was the Messiah they had been waiting for. When these Pharisee Christians heard about Paul's gentile converts, they said, "It is necessary to circumcise them, and to charge them to keep the law of Moses," conditions that would apply to any convert to Judaism (Acts 15:5). The account of Paul's later and final visit to Jerusalem is revealing about what many Christian Jews thought of Paul's message:

> When we [Paul and his companions] had come to Jerusalem, the brethren received us gladly. On the following day Paul went in with us to James [the brother of Jesus]; and all the elders were present. After greeting them, he related one by one the things that God had done among the Gentiles through his ministry. And when they heard it, they glorified God. And they said to him, "You see, brother, how many thousands there are among the Jews of those who have believed; *they are all zealous for the law, and they have been told about you that you teach all the Jews who are among the Gentiles to forsake Moses, telling them not to circumcise their children or observe the customs.* What then is to be done? They will certainly hear that you have come." (Acts 21:17–22, RSV, emphasis added)

James and the elders were concerned that their Jewish Christian converts were very upset about Paul's lax attitude toward the law of Moses. It was not the decision to convert gentiles they were concerned about, or even the idea of exempting gentile converts from the Jewish laws. People were upset because Paul was telling Christian Jews to stop following the Jewish laws, so they could fellowship with gentiles. It is clear that Paul did do this, from the passage quoted previously where he was angry at Peter and Barnabas over this very thing (Gal. 2:9–16). The concern of James and the elders turned out to be warranted. On their advice, Paul went to the temple to perform some rituals to show that he followed the law, but this did not placate his Jewish opponents. There may have been both Christian and non-Christian Jews who were concerned about Paul's message, but it was not belief in Jesus they were upset about in this case, it was Paul's position on the Jewish law:

> Jews from Asia [Asia Minor, Galatia], who had seen him in the temple, stirred up all the crowd, and laid hands on him, crying out,

---

4. Josephus, *Antiquities* 20.9.1.

"Men of Israel, help! This is the man *who is teaching men everywhere against the people and the law and this place*; moreover he also brought Greeks into the temple, and he has defiled this holy place." For they had previously seen Trophimus the Ephesian with him in the city, and they supposed that Paul had brought him into the temple. Then all the city was aroused, and the people ran together; they seized Paul and dragged him out of the temple, and at once the gates were shut. And as they were trying to kill him, word came to the [Roman] tribune of the cohort that all Jerusalem was in confusion. He at once took soldiers and centurions, and ran down to them; and when they saw the tribune and the soldiers, they stopped beating Paul. Then the tribune came up and arrested him, and ordered him to be bound with two chains. He inquired who he was and what he had done. Some in the crowd shouted one thing, some another; and as he could not learn the facts because of the uproar, he ordered him to be brought into the barracks. And when he came to the steps, he was actually carried by the soldiers because of the violence of the crowd; for the mob of the people followed, crying, "Away with him!" (Acts 21:27–36, RSV, emphasis added)

Although the book of Acts portrayed both James and Peter as supportive of Paul, this support did not include many of their followers. The conflicts related in the books of Acts and Galatians are examples of how the first Christians in Jerusalem viewed themselves. They were Jews through and through, Jews who thought they knew who the Jewish Messiah really was.

Outside of the New Testament, there are records of a continuing tradition of Jewish Christians who did not accept Paul's openness to gentiles.[5] These Christian Jews had their own written versions of the story of Jesus, were faithful to the Jewish ritual laws, and believed Jesus was a prophet and the Messiah but not God himself, similar to the way Jesus is portrayed in the Gospels of Mark and Matthew. An example of this is an early Christian document that claimed (falsely) to be a letter from Peter to James, and said that only a man who has been circumcised is a true believer.[6] In the New Testament, the Gospel of Matthew is the most supportive of the Jewish Christian point of view, with Jesus saying:

Do not think that I have come to abolish the law and the prophets . . .
Whoever breaks one of the least of these commandments and teaches men so, shall be called least in the kingdom of heaven; but

---

5. Ehrman, *Lost Christianities*, ch. 5; Levine, *Misunderstood Jew*, 84.

6. *Letter From Peter to James*, translated by Ehrman, *Lost Scriptures* 190–91.

he who does them and teaches them shall be called great in the kingdom of heaven. (Matt. 5:17, 19)

Was Matthew referring to the apostle Paul, who breaks the commandments and teaches men so? The author may have been expressing a compromise. He reprimanded Paul's position, but still allowed that Paul and his non-Jewish converts could be in the Kingdom of Heaven, although with lower status than observant Jews who are the true followers of Jesus.

A similar point of view is found in the Didache, or Teaching of the Twelve Apostles, previously discussed as one of the earliest Christian writings (chapter 7). Some historians have suggested it may have been written as advice to gentile converts.[7] A long section of moral instructions to refrain from sexual immorality, violence, greed, and "the way of death" is summed up in a passage that refers to the Jewish laws:

> For if you can bear the entire yoke of the Lord, you will be perfect;
> but if you cannot, do as much as you can. And concerning food,
> bear what you can. But especially abstain from food sacrificed to
> idols; for this is a ministry to dead gods. (Didache 6:1–3)

These instructions from the Didache echoed the position of James and the Jerusalem church as presented in the book of Acts. They and the Didache author preferred that gentile Christians keep the Jewish law (the entire yoke of the Lord), but did not demand it. Gentiles did not have to be circumcised. The instruction to avoid food sacrificed to idols referred to the common practice of sacrificing animals to a pagan god, then selling the meat in the markets. Eating this meat was a controversial issue for early Christians, discussed by Paul in two of his letters (Rom. 14; 1 Cor. 8). Abstaining from these foods was one of the instructions in the letter given to Paul by the Jerusalem Christians for his gentile converts (Acts 15:19–35).

Though they disagreed with Paul about the importance of the Jewish laws, in Paul's letters and everything else in the New Testament there is no evidence that the first Jewish Christians or Jesus' own disciples disagreed with Paul about other aspects of the Christian message such as Jesus as the Messiah, the importance of the Holy Spirit, or the imminent end of the age. The disciples of Jesus were surprised to find their message taking on a life of its own, spreading to non-Jews as it was promoted by the enigmatic apostle Paul. He formerly had persecuted them, but then challenged them to change their understanding of what it meant to follow Jesus.

---

7. Pagels, *Beyond Belief*, 15–18.

10

Christianity in the Roman World

ROMANS AND CHRISTIANS

Apart from the writings of Josephus, there is very little to fill out the story of Jesus and the first Christians from writings outside the Bible. The Roman historian Tacitus (about 115 CE) reported that in 64 CE the Emperor Nero had parts of Rome burned to make way for new construction. When people suspected Nero was behind the fire, he blamed Christians. He rounded up many Christians and tortured and executed them in creative ways. Tacitus remarked that this made some people pity them, though they still deserved it, not for the fire but because they were Christians. He described Christianity as an anti-social superstition, giving a glimpse of what many Romans thought of Christians, stemming from the Christians' unwillingness to honor the Emperor as a god.[1] Tacitus provided few historical facts about Christians, saying only that Jesus had been executed during the reign of Tiberias by Pilate the governor of Judea. Tradition has it that Peter and Paul were martyred during this persecution of Christians by Nero in 64 CE. One significant historical fact from this report by Tacitus is that Christians were recognized as a sect in Rome independent from Jews by the 60s CE, allowing Nero to single them out for persecution.

Another early reference to Christians is from 112 CE, in a letter written by Pliny the Younger to the Roman Emperor Trajan.[2] Pliny the Younger (so called to distinguish him from his famous uncle, the philosopher Pliny

---

1. Tacitus, *Annals*, XV.44, translated by Barrett, *New Testament Background*, 15–16.

2. B. M. Peper and M. DelCogliano, "The Pliny and Trajan Correspondence," 366–371 in Levine et al., *Historical Jesus*.

the Elder) was governor of a Roman province in what is now northwestern Turkey. Christians came to his attention because of a Roman policy forbidding social gatherings or societies, a policy intended to prevent uprisings. Pliny knew that Christians had been punished before, and asked Trajan for guidance: Should the young be treated differently from adults? Should a pardon be granted for recanting and renouncing Christianity? Should the name and self-identification as Christian be punished when no crimes (such as illegal assembly) had been committed, or should only the crimes be punished?

In his letter, Pliny described what he had been doing with some people who were accused of being Christians. An anonymous list had surfaced naming a large number of people as Christians. He asked them if they were Christian under threat of punishment. They were required to pay homage to the statue of the Emperor, and curse Christ. If they refused to recant they were executed. His comment on this is illuminating: "I did this because I had no doubt that, whatever else they were confessing, stubbornness and unyielding obstinacy warranted punishment." Apparently these were locals and not Roman citizens, because others "who were beset with a similar insanity" but were Roman citizens he did not execute, but sent to "the city" (Rome?) for trial. These actions have parallels with the treatment of Paul in the Acts of the Apostles. Paul was arrested for being involved in a disturbance (see chapter 9), and, facing scourging during questioning, he informed the Roman tribune holding him that he was a Roman citizen (Acts 22:24–29). This resulted in better treatment. Later, after Paul appealed to the Emperor he was sent to Rome for trial (Acts 25:12).

Pliny the Younger was concerned about the growing popularity of Christianity, reporting in his letter to Trajan that "the infection of this superstition" had spread not only through the towns, but also the villages and countryside. He said the pagan temples had been nearly abandoned, but thanks to his crackdown many Christians had recanted and returned to the traditional temples and rites. He thought the matter was worthy of bringing to the emperor because of the large number of people brought to trial, including people of every age and rank, and both sexes. He investigated the activities of these Christians, and some told him what they had been doing:

> . . . the sum total of their guilt was nothing more than that they regularly assembled on a fixed day before dawn to sing antiphonally a hymn to Christ as a god, and also to bind themselves by an oath, not to any criminal act, but rather not to steal, rob, or

commit adultery, not to deceive the trust of another person, and not to refuse to return a debt. After this, it was their custom to disperse and then reassemble again for a meal that was of a common and harmless nature.[3]

This description of Christian activities is consistent with an account by the church leader Justin, writing about 150 CE, several decades after the letter of Pliny. He was traveling from Asia Minor to Rome, and described what Christians did in the various groups he visited:

> All those who live in the city or the country gather together in one place on the day of the sun, and memoirs of the apostles or the writings of the prophets are read. . . . Then we all rise together and pray, and then . . . bread and wine are brought [to be shared].[4]

Justin added that the gathering was on Sunday because that was the day Jesus rose from the dead, having been crucified (he said) the day before.

Paul also mentioned this practice of gathering for a meal which he called the Lord's supper, or the bread and cup of the Lord (1 Cor. 11:17–34). This was the familiar Christian ritual of bread and wine, done in remembrance of Jesus. It was not a simple, individual ritual as observed in modern churches, but was more of a shared meal and time of fellowship.[5] Paul was concerned about the way it was being done; some were eating too much while others were going hungry. He gave this "Lord's supper" profound spiritual significance, saying that the abuse of it was the reason some of them were sick and some had died. The Didache also gave instructions for this shared meal, an important ritual for early Christians that came to be called Eucharist, a Greek word that literally means "thanksgiving." This may have been taken from the ritual sayings, as Paul says he heard it: "The Lord Jesus on the night he was betrayed took bread, and when he had given thanks [Greek *eucharisteo*], he broke it, and said, 'This is my body which is broken for you. Do this in remembrance of me'" (1 Cor. 11:22–23).

This meal gathering had drawn the attention of Pliny following the Emperor's order banning organized societies. Determined to do his duty and get to the bottom of the matter, Pliny "interrogated two slave women called deaconesses, to find out the truth, using torture." What he found was

---

3. Translation based on B. M. Peper and M. DelCogliano, "The Pliny and Trajan Correspondence," 366–371 in Levine et al., *Historical Jesus*.

4. Justin, *Apology I*, 67, translation from Pagels, *Beyond Belief*, 24.

5. On the meaning of the ritual see Pagels, *Beyond Belief*, 17–27.

"nothing more than a depraved and fanatical superstition." He was hopeful that with enough pressure he could stamp it out.

A few things stand out from this letter of Pliny the Younger to Trajan in 112 CE. Pliny was aware of precedent for punishing Christians. Also, Christianity had spread and was successful enough that Pliny thought it was a threat to traditional Roman religious practices, pulling people away from the Roman temples. Christians worshiped Christ as a god, and were committed to a code of personal conduct that had some things in common with the Ten Commandments. They met for a communal meal, they were from all walks of life, and two of their respected members were women. Not only that, these "deaconesses" were slave women!

Though it is a harsh reality, there is something poignant and powerful in this image of the bureaucrat Pliny dutifully arresting and torturing some poor slave women to find out what mischief these Christians might be up to, and not really finding anything except that they worshiped Christ, were committed to doing good, and were remarkably stubborn about denying their faith. The Emperor Trajan wrote back thoughtfully to say, "Pliny, you acted correctly with those accused of being Christians. Punish them unless they recant and sacrifice to our gods, but do not seek them out, and do not arrest people on hearsay or anonymous charges, because that sets a dangerous precedent." Meanwhile, these slave women and their friends rose before dawn to sing a hymn to Christ—a Jew who was executed—as to a god. What did they sing? What scriptures, stories and teachings did they have and cherish? What did they believe, that they would endure torture rather than deny their faith, and how did they come to this faith?

ROMAN RELIGION AND THE SON OF GOD

In the letter of Pliny the Younger are glimpses of how the Romans understood religion, and what they thought of Christianity. They did not necessarily object to the belief that Christ was a god. It was the exclusivity of the belief that bothered them, the assertion by Christians that only Jesus should be worshiped—not Zeus, Apollo, Isis, or Caesar, or any of the gods that were intertwined with Roman culture.

By the time of Pliny the Younger in the early second century CE, Christianity was changing to look less like a messianic Jewish sect and more like a Roman religion or mystery cult, of which there were many, some remarkably similar to Christianity in its Roman form.[6] Gods such as Isis and Asclepius were believed to interact with individuals in a personal and compassionate way.[7] Despite a general openness to many gods, a person might be principally devoted to one of the gods. The popular Mithras cult had initiation rites that included showering the initiate with the blood of a bull, and eating a shared ritual meal. Devotees were promised blessings in this life and the afterlife. Mithras was associated with the sun, and was reborn every December 25th at the winter solstice.[8] After Christianity supplanted these gods, December 25th was celebrated as the birthday of Christ.

A second century Roman novel[9] identified Isis as the God of all gods and goddesses. She described herself as "she whose deity the whole world worships in different ways, by various rites, and by many names."[10] Isis saved Lucius, the protagonist of the story, from his troubles, and he devoted himself to her service. His initiation ritual was said to be a voluntary death and rebirth. Lucius praised Isis with a devotion matching that of passages of worship from the Bible:

> Most holy and everlasting savior of the human race, always gener-
> ously cherishing our lives, you who always give the sweet affection
> of a loving mother to the troubles of the miserable . . .
>
> My spirit cannot give you enough praise, and I have not the
> goods to give you sufficient offering. My voice is not strong enough
> to say what I think of your majesty, not even if I had a thousand
> mouths and tongues and an eternal flow of words. . . . I will do
> what I am able, a religious person with poor estate. I will imagine
> your divine face within my breast, and there, in the secret depths,
> I will guard your most holy divinity forever.[11]

The story of Lucius and Isis, and similar accounts, show that the idea of a personal relationship with a loving supreme God was familiar to Romans, providing a natural connection to the message of Christians about the risen Jesus Christ and his Holy Spirit.

---

6. Harris, *New Testament*, ch. 3; Levine et al., *Historical Jesus*, ch. 9, 10, 11.

7. Cartlidge and Dungan, *Documents for the Study of the Gospels*, 165–68.

8. Harris, *New Testament*, 43; M. Meyer, "The Mithras Liturgy," 179–192 in Levine et al., *Historical Jesus*.

9. Apuleius, *The Metamorphoses*, or *Golden Ass*; see I. Henderson, "Apuleius of Mad-auros," 193–205 in Levine et al., *Historical Jesus*.

10. Apuleius, *Metamorphoses* Book 11, translation from Cartlidge and Dungnan, *Documents for the Study of the Gospels*, p. 167–8.

11. Ibid.

There were also important differences between Roman religion and the Jewish heritage of Christianity. To illustrate these differences, the phrase "son of God" is a helpful example. Jesus was called "the son of God" in the Gospels (Mark 1:1, for example). Jewish and non-Jewish audiences probably would have understood this differently. For Jews, a son of God meant someone who had a special relationship with God; it did not mean the person was God himself or was literally God's son. In some Jewish scriptures, "son of God" referred to an angel or heavenly being (Job 1:6), but in Psalm 2, God called the human King of Israel "son": "You are my son, today I have begotten you." Christians used this as a prophecy of the Messiah (Heb. 1:5, 5:5), and called Jesus "the only begotten son of God" (John 3:17). The meaning is that Jesus is in a special relationship to God, he is the Messiah and the most important son of God, but God is not literally his physical father, nor is he equal to God. The Qumran (Dead Sea Scrolls) community also called the expected Messiah King "the son of God," but there is no evidence they thought this person would actually be divine himself.[12]

References to the Messiah as the son of God may be connected to an Old Testament prophecy given to King David of Israel, in which God said he would raise up a son of David as king, and "I will be his father and he will be my son," and his kingdom will be established forever (2 Sam. 7:13–14). Clearly, this son of David, the Messiah, would be a human king and descendent of David yet God called him "son." The phrase "Jesus the Christ, the son of God" (Mark 1:2, John 20:31) may be a reference to this fact that "Son of God" was another title used for the Messiah, the Christ, who would also be a son of David.

Non-Jewish people hearing that Jesus was the son of God probably would have had a different idea. A son of a god might be a person with special powers, but it often meant that a god literally was the person's father. There were various sons of gods in Greek and Roman legend, such as Heracles (Hercules), son of Zeus and a human mother. Caesar Augustus, Emperor at the time of Jesus' birth, was supposed to be the son of Apollo who came to his mother as she slept in a temple. He was called "the son of a god" (Latin *divi filius*) on his coins.[13] Apollonius of Tyana was the result of divine intervention when the god Proteus came to his mother while she was pregnant.

---

12. P. Flint, "Jesus and the Dead Sea Scrolls," 110–131 in Levine et al., *Historical Jesus*; Schiffman, *Reclaiming the Dead Sea Scrolls*, 341–44.

13. C. Talbert, "Miraculous Conceptions and Births in Mediterranean Antiquity," 79–86 in Levine et al., *Historical Jesus*; Crossan and Reed, *Excavating Jesus*, 85–88, 177.

Another son of Apollo and a human mother was Asclepius, who became a god of healing. It was said that during his mortal life, he was a great healer with unusual power, even raising people from the dead. He had a reputation for great compassion for all, regardless of social status. He was killed at the order of Zeus because he was saving too many people from death, but he lived on as a god with a devoted following throughout the Roman empire.[14] Miracles of healing were believed to happen for those who slept in his temples.

There are obvious parallels between Asclepius, Apollonius and Jesus: all three were compassionate, miracle-working, sons of gods. This is how Roman listeners probably would have understood the Christian message—if Jesus was the son of the Jewish god, then that god was literally his father. Christians needed a miraculous birth story for Jesus, like Asclepius and other sons of gods, and this was provided by the story of the virgin birth when the Spirit of God impregnated Mary. The Gospel of Luke tells the story:

> And Mary said to the angel, "How shall this be, since I have no husband?" And the angel said to her, "The Holy Spirit will come upon you, and the power of the Most High will overshadow you; therefore the child to be born will be called holy, the Son of God." (Luke 1:35, RSV)

Josephus told a story that illustrates the way a Roman audience might have understood the idea of a son of a god.[15] It is a tale of obsession, sex and intrigue suitable for a Hollywood movie. It happened during the reign of Emperor Tiberius, 14–37 CE. Paulina was a wealthy, beautiful Roman woman. She had a reputation as virtuous and modest, married to a respectable man named Saturninus. Paulina was devoted to the goddess Isis, at the Temple of Isis in Rome. Decius Mundus, a high officer in the Roman cavalry, fell in love with Paulina and thought he had to have her. She rejected his advances even when he offered her a large sum of money for just one night together. The lovesick Mundus then decided he would starve himself to death. His servant woman Ide, who had served his father's family for many years, intervened and promised Mundus she could get him a night with Paulina, and for much less money than he had offered. She went to the Isis temple and bribed some priests to help her. The eldest priest went to Paulina and told her that he had been sent by the god Anubis, son of Isis. The

---

14. W. Cotter, "Miracle Stories," 168 in Levine et al., *Historical Jesus.*

15. Josephus, *Antiquities,* 18.3.4.

priest said Anubis had fallen in love with Paulina and wanted her to come to the temple to spend the night with him. Paulina, apparently as gullible as she was devout, was flattered by the news and told her husband about it. He trusted her and they agreed to accept the offer. People did not believe all the legends about the gods, but they did believe the gods were real and such things were within the realm of possibility, just as they believed that Asclepius could work miracles of healing or be raised from the dead.

Paulina went to the temple, and after supper the priest shut the doors and put out the lights. Mundus came out of hiding impersonating Anubis and spent the night with Paulina in the temple. Paulina went home and excitedly told her husband how the god Anubis had appeared to her. She probably hoped she would get pregnant with the son of a god. She also told her friends about this great honor. They found it hard to believe but did not think Paulina would lie about a thing like that.

A few days later, Mundus met Paulina and bragged to her about what he had done. She was furious and humiliated. Her husband reported it to the Emperor Tiberius, who investigated and confirmed the story. He then ordered the priests and the servant woman who bribed them to be crucified. As further punishment for this abuse of position and public trust, he demolished the Temple of Isis in Rome and had the statue of Isis thrown into the river! Perhaps this was intended to punish the goddess, or the whole institution of Isis? The man who caused the whole thing, Mundus, got off relatively easily with banishment from Rome, because the Emperor saw it as a crime of passion. This story shows something of the relationship between Romans and their gods, and how seriously they took the temples and priests, and how literally they might have understood the meaning of "the son of god."

It would have been no stretch of the imagination for a Roman to believe that a son of a god such as Jesus, Asclepius, or the Emperor could perform healings or other miracles. Tacitus (c.115 CE), the Roman historian who told of Nero's persecution of Christians, relayed a story of a healing miracle that involved the Emperor Vespasian, the conqueror of Jerusalem and patron of Josephus. This very human story illustrates the common belief that signs and wonders would naturally accompany the Emperor, even though he is human and may be uncertain of his power. The author Tacitus was writing about forty years after the events he described, and he clearly believed the story to be true:

> During the months while Vespasian was waiting at Alexandria for
> the regular season of the summer winds and a settled sea, many

marvels occurred to mark the favor of heaven and the partiality of the gods toward him. One of the common people of Alexandria, well known for his blindness, threw himself at Vespasian's knees, and implored him with groans to heal his blindness. This he did by the advice of the god Serapis, whom this nation, devoted as it is to many superstitions, worships more than any other god. He begged Vespasian to deign to moisten his cheeks and eyes with his spittle. Another whose hand was useless, prompted by the same god, begged Caesar to step on his injured hand. At first Vespasian ridiculed these appeals and treated them with scorn. Then, when the men persisted, he on the one hand feared the discredit of failure, yet, on the other, was filled with hopes of success by the appeals of the supplicants and the flattery of his courtiers. At last he directed the physicians to give their opinion whether such blindness and infirmity could be overcome by human aid. They discussed the matter from different points of view. . . . Such perhaps was the wish of the gods, and the Emperor might be chosen for this divine service. In any case, all the glory of a successful remedy would be Caesar's, while the ridicule of failure would fall on the poor supplicants. So Vespasian, believing that his good fortune was capable of anything and that nothing was any longer past belief, with a joyful face, amid the intense expectation of the bystanders, did as he was asked. The hand was instantly restored to its use, and the light of day again shone for the blind man. Both facts are told by eyewitnesses even now when nothing is to be gained by lying.[16]

This story of Vespasian, and similar stories of other healers, provide some cultural context for the miracle stories about Jesus, and how people understood them. There were miracle stories about other famous philosophers and holy men, such as Pythagoras.[17] Jewish prophets and rabbis also were known to work miracles, such as Elijah in the Old Testament, and a rabbi from near the time of Jesus named Honi. The idea of Jesus as a miracle-working son of God was not as unique in the eyes of people of his time as we might think with our modern view of the world. Factual or not, it would have been strange if Jesus had not had any miracle stories, given what people expected from divine heroes.

---

16. Tacitus, *Histories* 4.81, translation based on W. Cotter, "Miracle Stories," 176 in Levine et al., *Historical Jesus*.

17. W. Cotter, "Miracle Stories," 168–78 in Levine et al., *Historical Jesus*; Cartlidge and Dungan, *Documents for the Study of the Gospels*, 151–64.

11

Constantine and the Nicene Creed

THE EDICT OF MILAN AND THE COUNCIL AT NICAEA

Persecution of Christians by the Romans began with Nero in 64 CE, and waxed and waned over the next 250 years. During this time, Christianity spread throughout Roman society and became more established despite persecution, but remained a small minority. The worst persecution began in the reign of Diocletian (reigned 284–305), and continued after his reign, with imprisonments and executions of Christian leaders and seizures of property. In 312, the new Emperor Constantine declared that he had converted to Christianity. As his biographer Eusebius of Caesarea told the story, Constantine was facing a decisive battle with a rival for control of the empire, and was seeking help from the supreme god, probably the sun god with which he and his father were associated. He had a dream in which Christ told him to use the sign of the cross to conquer his enemies. He did this and attributed his subsequent victory and control of the empire to Christ, thereafter declaring his allegiance to Christianity. In 313 he issued the Edict of Milan which officially ended the persecution of Christians, and declared that all, pagans and Christians, were free to worship as they pleased. He did not outlaw Roman temples and practices, and he continued his association with the sun god, but began actively supporting Christianity.[1]

It is one of the ironies and shames of history that after Constantine ended the persecution of Christians and gave them the power of the state, they persecuted each other. Christians had been bickering for a long time

---

1. Ehrman, *Lost Christianities*, Pagels, *Beyond Belief*; Rubenstein, *When Jesus Became God*; Drake, *Constantine and the Bishops*.

over differences of doctrine and practice. By the fourth century CE, there was a well-established network of Christian leaders who called themselves "orthodox," meaning "correct." They called anyone they disagreed with "heretics," which literally meant that they believed differently, but which came to be a pejorative term for people the orthodox considered unbelievers and deceivers. This included gnostics, Jewish Christians who kept the Jewish law, and other Christians who deviated from the opinions of the orthodox. Among bishops who were part of this network there were bitter disagreements over differences of doctrine that could appear utterly trivial even to other Christians. These fights were part religious debate and part political power struggle, as rival bishops vied for powerful leadership positions.

Eventually, power was centralized in the Roman church and all other Christian leaders were subordinated to the Bishop of Rome, a position that became the Roman Catholic Pope. This resulted in greater unity in Christian doctrine, and the elimination of much of the diversity that had grown since the time of the first apostles. Today, even with all the variety of Christian beliefs, most Christian churches base their beliefs on this unified version of Christianity that emerged as dominant in the late fourth century. These churches accept the Nicene Creed, a statement of beliefs adopted by church leaders in 325 CE as a way to decide who was part of the "true" church supported by Rome, and who was not. It is worth considering how this happened.

After Constantine decided to support Christianity, he contacted prominent bishops throughout the empire and invited them to a council to iron out their differences, to be held in 325 CE at the town of Nicaea.[2] Constantine told the bishops that he thought God had appointed him bishop of those outside the church. He wanted a unified church that he could support with the power and wealth of the state. He was frustrated with all the bickering and urged the bishops to restore harmony to the faith. Constantine had already begun sending money to bishops for construction of churches and support for the poor, and had exempted clergy from taxes. He required restitution to churches whose property had been seized in the recent persecutions. These benefits were only for those who were ministers of what he called "the lawful and most holy catholic religion." He had written an

---

2. For a summary see Pagels, *Beyond Belief*, ch. 5; For full discussion of Constantine and the Council of Nicaea see Rubenstein, *When Jesus Became God*; Drake, *Constantine and the Bishops*.

order specifying not only this limitation of benefits, but also that "heretics and schismatics" be imprisoned with compulsory public service. It was of vital importance to distinguish insiders from outsiders, and considerable political power was at stake.

The main point of contention at the Council of Nicaea was what came to be known as the Arian Controversy, named after a popular Libyan priest named Arius. Eusebius of Caesarea, who was present at the council, reported that the matter caused much consternation. Constantine probably did not care much about the outcome of the debate, he just wanted an agreement. He had said in his invitational letter that he thought they should be able to accept some minor differences in things so hard to understand. He warned that they must not allow their divisiveness to give the devil the victory that their persecutors had been unable to win by force.

Arius taught that Jesus Christ, the Word of God and Son of God, is divine but not in the same way as God the Father. He came from the Father, and so is not equal with the Father. The Arian doctrine might seem unremarkable to many Christians today, as it did in Arius' time. Many bishops, particularly in the eastern part of the empire, agreed with Arius that Christ was subordinate to and not exactly the same as God the Father; they were called "subordinationists." The conflict was driven by Alexander, Bishop of Alexandria in Egypt. He heard about what Arius was teaching, and in 318 CE convened a council of Egyptian bishops to declare Arius a heretic and excommunicate him, along with any priests who sided with him. This ignited a controversy, including riots and street battles in Alexandria, between factions supporting each side. Other bishops convened their own councils, some reinstating Arius and declaring his teaching to be faithful to the gospel. The controversy and riots spread to Antioch, one of the other great Christian centers, over the appointment of a new bishop there. Many bishops urged Alexander to back down—surely there was room for some difference of opinion on these obtuse matters—but he refused. Arius refused to recant his position.

Alexander was assisted by his young secretary Athanasius, later to succeed Alexander as bishop. This was the same Athanasius who later, in 367 CE, issued the list of approved Christian books that became the New Testament (see chapter 7). Alexander and Athanasius declared that Christ was entirely equal to and pre-existent with God, with no qualifications, and anything else was heresy—a position that excluded a large number of Christians both at that time and before, including some prominent church leaders and theologians. Alexander and Athanasius arrived at the Council of Nicaea in 325 determined to win the argument and excommunicate any who disagreed, including Arius and his supporters. The Arians were hoping to win the day by accepting their opponents as part of the same church, which they knew was consistent with Constantine's goal for the conference. In the end, Alexander and his supporters would not budge. A frustrated Constantine broke the deadlock by supporting Alexander against Arius. Most bishops succumbed to the pressure and signed the Nicene Creed even if they disagreed, under threat of excommunication, which was the fate of Arius and a few others who did not sign. Constantine's former advisor (and our historian) Eusebius of Caesarea, who had made the opening speech at the meeting, signed the creed but later wrote a letter saying he did not interpret it to mean Jesus was equal to God the Father. This infuriated Alexander and resulted in the excommunication of Eusebius.

Everyone at the council, as far as we know, agreed on a statement that Christ was "made man," to counter gnostics and other docetic Christians who said Christ was not really human. The main point of the Nicene Creed, however, was that Jesus was fully God, "of one substance" with the Father. The original creed was shorter than the one familiar today, because it was expanded and revised in 381. The original Nicene Creed of 325 CE, quoted below, ended with some additional anti-Arian statements that were removed from the later version:

> We believe in one God, the Father Almighty, Maker of all things visible and invisible.
>
> And in one Lord Jesus Christ, the Son of God, begotten of the Father, the only-begotten; that is, of the essence of the Father, God of God, Light of Light, very God of very God, begotten, not made, being of one substance with the Father; by whom all things were made both in heaven and on earth; who for us men, and for our salvation, came down and was incarnate and was made man; he suffered, and the third day he rose again, ascended into heaven; from thence he shall come to judge the quick and the dead.
>
> And in the Holy Ghost.
>
> But those who say: "There was a time when he was not;" and "He was not before he was made;" and "He was made out of nothing," or "He is of another substance" or "essence," or "The Son of God is created," or "changeable," or "alterable"—they are condemned by the holy catholic and apostolic Church.[3]

---

3. Nicene Creed of 325 CE, translation from Schaff, *Creeds of Christendom*.

I AND THE FATHER ARE ONE

Most of the Nicene Creed emphasized that Jesus was equal to and pre-existent with God, while his incarnation as man got only passing mention. Likewise, many Christians today and in history have paid only lip service to the idea that Jesus was fully human, as much of his humanity has been trumped by his divinity. Like the bishops gathered at the council of Nicaea, Christians traditionally have allowed that Jesus could be tempted, and suffer and die, but not that he ever was less than all-knowing, all-powerful, holy and perfect. His apparently was just a token humanity. To this way of thinking, he could never have been unaware, or mistaken, or have done anything wrong, or felt lost or powerless, all of which are characteristics of humans. When on the cross Jesus cried out, "My God, my God, why have you forsaken me?" (Mark 15:34), was he was just quoting Psalm 22 for our benefit, or did he really mean it? When in great distress he prayed to God for the cup of crucifixion to pass from him (Mark 14:32–36), was he praying to himself? I recently heard a preacher say that Jesus had to be tempted directly by the devil himself (Matt. 4) because he was so perfect that he could not be tempted by his human nature like the rest of us. Such an exalted Jesus is impossible to "follow" as he commanded.

People on both sides of the Arian controversy argued strenuously that they, and they alone, represented the true and original version of Christianity, as taught by the apostles. The argument centered around two key passages: the first chapter of the Gospel of John, and Paul's letter to the Philippians. Of the four Gospels, John most clearly presents Jesus as divine, while in the Gospel of Mark he is clearly human. Matthew and Luke are in the middle, sometimes softening the humanity of Jesus while incorporating Mark. For example, in the story of the woman healed by touching the garment of Jesus (Mark 5:25–34), Mark says that Jesus asked "Who touched me?" In Matthew (9:20–22), this question is missing, and the woman was healed only after Jesus addressed her directly. Perhaps the author did not want to portray Jesus as unaware, so he cut this line. I have heard preachers say that Jesus of course knew who touched him, he was just giving the woman a chance to come forward. I think it is clear that this pious interpretation was not the intent of the author of the Gospel of Mark.

The humanity of Jesus also featured in the story of the rich young man who asked Jesus what he must do to be saved (Mark 10:17–22). He called Jesus "Good master," out of respect, but Jesus responded, "Why do you call me good? There is no one good but God." Jesus was saying that he was not equal with God. The Jesus of Mark is the Son of God and the Christ, but not equal to God himself.

The Gospel of John, in contrast, begins with a passage identifying Jesus Christ as the *logos* of God, the divine Word of God that created everything:

> In the beginning was the Word, and the Word was with God, and the Word was God.
>
> He was in the beginning with God; all things were made through him, and without him was not anything made that was made. In him was life, and the life was the light of men. The light shines in the darkness, and the darkness has not overcome it . . .
>
> He was in the world, and the world was made through him, yet the world knew him not. He came to his own home, and his own people received him not. But to all who received him, who believed in his name, he gave power to become children of God; who were born, not of blood nor of the will of the flesh nor of the will of man, but of God.
>
> And the Word became flesh and dwelt among us, full of grace and truth; we beheld his glory, glory as of the only Son from the Father. (John 1:1–14, RSV)

John equates Jesus with the Word, and the Word with God. Unlike the other Gospels where Jesus does not identify himself as God, in the Gospel of John he says "I and the Father are one," and "before Abraham was, I am," apparently taking the sacred name of God (I Am, or Yahweh, Exod. 3:14) for himself. People who heard him understood it this way, taking up stones to kill him for blasphemy (John 8:58, 59). Also in the Gospel of John, Thomas calls the risen Jesus "My Lord and my God!" (John 20:28).

The Gospel of John, therefore, suggests the exalted view of Christ of the Nicene Creed. Even in John, however, Jesus prayed to the Father (not himself, the Arians pointed out) and said, "I do nothing on my own authority," and even more clearly, "the Father is greater than I" (John 5:19, 8:28, 12:49, 14:28). Except for this ambiguity in John, the Nicene Creed is not in agreement with the Gospels, or with the beliefs of Jews about the Messiah that were applied to Jesus. As Christianity spread and changed into a separate religion, the Jewish meaning of the Messiah developed into a diversity of beliefs about the divinity and humanity of Jesus the Christ. Some of this diversity is represented in the New Testament, allowing people to support different interpretations of Jesus depending on which passages they emphasize.

As for Paul, he said that God will exalt Christ over everything, but "the Son himself will be subjected to him who put all things under him, that God may be everything to everyone" (1 Cor. 15:28). He also said, "he who raised Christ Jesus from the dead will give life to your mortal bodies also through his Spirit which dwells in you," equating the Holy Spirit with God but not Christ Jesus (Rom. 8:11). From this and similar passages it is clear that Paul was on the side of Arius: Christ, the Son and Word of God, is subordinate to God the Father, however slightly.

One passage in Paul's letter to the Philippians was claimed by both sides in the Arian Controversy. These verses describe how Christ came into human form and sacrificed himself, for which he has been exalted:

> . . . Christ Jesus . . . though he was in the form of God, did not count equality with God a thing to be grasped, but emptied himself, taking the form of a servant, being born in the likeness of men. And being found in human form he humbled himself and became obedient unto death, even death on a cross. Therefore God has highly exalted him . . . that at the name of Jesus every knee should bow, in heaven and on earth and under the earth, and every tongue confess that Jesus Christ is Lord, to the glory of God the Father. (Phil. 2:5–11, RSV)

This passage may be a kind of hymn or creed that Paul got from other Christians. To appear in a letter by Paul it must have been in use very early, before the writing of the four Gospels. Christians have long said that this passage describes Christ Jesus as equal and pre-existent with God, but does it really say that? The point of it is that Christ Jesus humbled and subordinated himself to God, rather than exalting himself and grasping at equality with God. This verse certainly presents an exalted view of Christ, but supports the idea that he is in some way distinct from and subordinate to God.

One possible interpretation of this passage from Philippians is that Jesus, though born a human like Adam in the image and likeness of God (Gen. 1:26), unlike Adam did not grasp at equality with God. Adam and Eve disobeyed God and ate the fruit of the forbidden tree because it would make them "like God" (Gen. 3:5). They grasped at equality with God, bringing a curse on everyone as the result of sin. Instead of doing this, the human Jesus broke this pattern, humbling himself and obeying even unto death on the cross. Therefore, God has highly exalted him, and now he is an exalted heavenly being and Lord of all. This interpretation makes sense of this difficult passage and again does not require that Christ is the same as God.[4]

---

4. For various translations and interpretations of this passage, see Harris, *New Testament*, 24–25.

These different understandings of Jesus as human or divine may be significant, but this was not the substance of the debate over which Arius and Eusebius were excommunicated. They were not arguing that there were some things Jesus did not know, or that Jesus could have felt despair. The difference was far smaller, as both sides had an exalted view of Christ. The argument was simply over allowing that Christ's status as the Son allowed for some kind of difference, however small. In any practical sense the two sides were very close, almost indistinguishable to an outside observer such as Constantine. It was the insistence of Alexander and Athanasius to excommunicate those who disagreed that made it an important issue, as reflected in the explicit condemnation of Arians in the Nicene Creed of 325 CE.

THE ROMAN CHURCH

As a matter of history there is an important distinction between the message *of* Jesus—a Jew who taught that we are all children of a loving God and God's kingdom is at hand—versus the message *about* Jesus that became the religion of Christianity. According to the Gospels, Jesus told people to worship God, not himself. Jews did not allow worship as God of anyone but their God Yahweh, whom Jesus called Father. They believed in the existence of heavenly beings such as angels, the equivalent of "gods" in the way non-Jews used the term, but these were not to be worshiped. The Messiah was to be a powerful figure and should be honored as king, even the powerful, heavenly "Son of Man" of Daniel, but not worshiped as the one and only God who was the true source of all things.

Christians, some time after Jesus, began to worship Jesus Christ as God. Did this mean there were two gods? The tendency to understand this polytheistically can be seen in the report of Pliny the Younger that Christians sang a hymn to Christ "as a god" (see chapter 10). Christians such as Athanasius wanted to pre-empt the idea that they worshiped more than one god, by saying that Jesus, God the Father, and the Holy Spirit are exactly the same in every way—the Holy Trinity. They do not worship Christ as a god, they would say, they worship him because he is the one and only God.

The triumph of the absolute divinity of Christ at the Council of Nicaea was not the end of the story. Subsequent councils overturned the results of Nicaea, and Constantine reinstated Arius and Eusebius. Each side appealed to Constantine for support and he shifted back and forth. In general, the Arians sought acceptance of creeds both sides could sign allowing room for different interpretations, while Athanasius and his supporters rejected the Arians as heretics and enemies with whom any compromise was impossible. Charges of corruption and violence were hurled by both sides. Athanasius was excommunicated for instigation of excessive violence, then reinstated, more than once. As Constantine had warned at the Council of Nicaea, the power struggle between the Arian and anti-Arian parties became a smoldering civil war, dividing the empire east and west roughly along Latin and Greek cultural lines.

After the death of Constantine in 337, the Arian Controversy became part of the power struggles between competing Caesars. In 380 CE, Emperor Theodosius I carried out a purge of Arian bishops. Soon Arianism was outlawed and profession of Arian beliefs or possession of subordinationist writings were punishable by death! It seems that Theodosius missed the point of Christianity, but he is remembered in Christian tradition as a hero for his purges of heretics. These actions further consolidated the power of the church in Rome. Theodosius also outlawed traditional Roman religious practices. The turnabout was then complete, as Christians freely oppressed pagan worshipers and Christian "heretics" as ferociously as all Christians had formerly been persecuted. A very specific version of Christianity had conquered the Roman Empire. The seed of the gospel had grown into a giant tree covering the earth with its branches, but this tree may have been unrecognizable to the people who planted it 350 years earlier.

12

Putting It All Together

J esus of Nazareth, and John the Baptist before him, were Jewish prophets and teachers of righteousness. Jesus was baptized by John as a sign of devotion to God. After John was arrested, Jesus carried on their message: "The time is fulfilled and the Kingdom of God is at hand; repent, and believe the good news" (Mark 1:15). Like the Old Testament prophet Micah, they taught that God requires justice, mercy and humility (Micah 6:8). Love God, and love your neighbor as yourself, and you will fulfill the law of God. Sell your possessions and give to the poor and you will have treasure in heaven. Very soon, God's Messiah or Christ, the divine Son of Man spoken of by the prophet Daniel, will come to restore the nation of Israel and bring the Kingdom of Heaven on earth.

In addition to this message of hope and righteousness, Jesus was known for healings and miracles. He gathered disciples, some of whom had been followers of John, and they spread the message of the Kingdom of Heaven, soon to come in power. It is not clear whether Jesus actually claimed to be the Messiah or not, but there is evidence in the Gospels that he did say this. He told his disciples that they would rule over the restored twelve tribes of Israel. He proclaimed that the coming Kingdom was already beginning to arrive, and he was crucified by the Roman authorities for being called the King of the Jews (Mark 15:26–32, John 19:19–22).

There is no way to know for sure whether Jesus expected to be killed, or thought his death was part of the plan. According to the Gospels, he told his disciples he would die and then rise again but they did not understand until after it happened (Mark 9:31, John 2:18–22). He had the example of John the Baptist who was killed, so it would be reasonable to expect he would be killed as well. He taught that the resurrection of the dead, which he and the Pharisees expected, was at hand, so his death would soon be overcome. Maybe he thought he would die but then return with or as the messianic Son of Man, but it is hard to tell because the Gospels that tell this story are the product of decades of hindsight and interpretation. The New Testament writers argued that the Jewish scriptures foretold the suffering, death and resurrection of the Christ, but this was a new interpretation and not the way Jews typically interpreted their scriptures.

After Jesus was killed, his disciples believed they saw him alive and that he had been resurrected into a new spiritual existence, as they all would be changed someday. They proclaimed that he really was the Messiah, and the resurrection that would accompany the Kingdom of Heaven had already started, with Jesus. He was the "first fruits" of this resurrection (1 Cor. 15:23), but soon he would return to finish the work of transforming the earth into a paradise for God's children, those who do God's will. The mission of these first apostles, including Paul, was to bring people into the family of believers, and to create a community of faith and love while waiting for the Day of the Lord. As the first apostles died and the Jerusalem temple was destroyed without the predicted return of Christ, Christians adapted their message to focus more on living and dying in the present. They deferred the hope of a future Kingdom of God on earth, or abandoned it altogether, emphasizing the Kingdom within and among believers through the Holy Spirit.

As Christianity spread through the Roman Empire, it lost much of its Jewish roots and became more diverse and more similar to other Roman religions. This occurred naturally as people who were not Jews brought their own ideas and assumptions about the gods to their new belief in Jesus as the Son of God. The main source of conflict with Romans was the exclusivity of Christianity, rejecting worship of the Emperor and influencing people to abandon the traditional Roman gods, temples, and rituals. Eventually, after intense persecution by the Romans, a form of Christianity emerged as the official religion of the Roman Empire.

It may be difficult for some Christians to accept that the founders of Christianity were wrong about the imminent end of the world, but this is the clear result of a literal reading of the Bible. The traditional explanation is that the Bible writers did not mean it that way, and must have been referring to the distant future. For example, when Jesus said it would happen in "this generation," he must have meant one last generation after some other conditions are fulfilled; after all, he said he did not know the exact time it would happen. When he said that some standing there would still be alive when it happened, he must have been talking about his resurrection or transfiguration or something else that happened at that time. These conclusions are guided by the assumption that the New Testament writers could not have meant what they clearly said and believed. Rather than a literal reading of the Bible, this adds a layer of interpretation on top of what the Bible actually says, on the principle that the Bible and Jesus must be perfect and infallible.

Some Christians take another approach, downplaying or denying the apocalyptic roots of the Christian message. They may embrace the idea that Jesus was not really apocalyptic, he was just portrayed that way. To do this, they must deny much of what the authors of the New Testament believed and said. The message of Paul and the first apostles was wrapped up in a vision of the imminent end of the age that they believed would happen in their lifetime. The Bible says Jesus also taught this, but even if he did not, it is clear that his followers did. They were wrong about this. The Kingdom of Heaven they expected did not come with power in their time or any time since. This means that the writings of the New Testament were wrong in part of their message, that the Day of the Lord was soon to come. This must be taken into account to understand them, and probably should be considered when applying their teachings to the lives of people living, raising families, and dying generation after generation.

The Bible was written by fallible human beings and is not a perfect book, but Christianity does not stand or fall on this doctrine. Biblical infallibility was never the point of Christian faith. Jesus and his followers emphasized faith, hope, and love for one another as the characteristics of those who know and follow the way of God. The New Testament did not yet exist when Jesus walked the earth, but grew out of their message and influence. Perfect or not, the New Testament is our primary connection to Jesus, his disciples and the movement they began.

The New Testament documents show that belief in the resurrection of Jesus originated with the first Christians. The risen Jesus was no longer a mere human being in these stories, though he had a real body and could eat food. He appeared and disappeared, and sometimes they did not recognize him. He had been resurrected into a new heavenly existence. In the earliest written account of the resurrection of Jesus, the apostle Paul related the story as it was told to him:

> For I delivered to you as of first importance what I also received, that Christ died for our sins in accordance with the scriptures, that he was buried, that he was raised on the third day in accordance with the scriptures, and that he appeared to Cephas [Peter], then to the twelve. Then he appeared to more than five hundred brethren at one time, most of whom are still alive, though some have fallen asleep [died]. Then he appeared to James [brother of Jesus], then to all the apostles. Last of all, as to one untimely born, he appeared also to me. (1 Cor. 15:3–10, RSV)

Paul had a mystical vision of Jesus (Acts 9:1–9), yet in this passage he equated his encounter with the risen Jesus with that of the original witnesses of the resurrection. Like the Gospel writers, Paul said that Jesus after his resurrection was not like he was before; he had been transformed. Paul believed that Jesus was alive in a new "spiritual body" (1 Cor. 15:42–54). This body was not flesh and blood, because "flesh and blood cannot inherit the Kingdom of Heaven." Similarly, Jesus taught that in "the resurrection" people would be "like the angels," not in normal physical bodies (Matt. 22:30). Paul believed that Jesus was already in that resurrected body after God raised him from the dead, and soon the rest of us will join him.

Paul also believed that God was guiding him through the Holy Spirit, and that anyone can experience this personally. We are invited to seek this same Spirit that inspired the disciples of Jesus to love one another and hope in God, bringing God's kingdom already on earth through compassion, forgiveness, and sharing, wherever two or three are gathered together (Matt. 18:20). Many people have rediscovered this Spirit in the story and teachings of Jesus and his followers, as I did when I began reading the Bible. I found a light and truth that transcended centuries of time and vast differences in culture. The Spirit of love that drew me to Jesus continues to speak to me from the pages of the Bible, a thread that runs through and unites the New Testament. This Spirit links people today with the first followers of Jesus, such as Paul who wrote, "faith, hope and love remain, these three; but the greatest is love. Make love your goal" (1 Cor. 13:13—14:1).

It is my hope that by understanding the context in which Jesus and his followers lived, some of the mists of time and centuries of interpretation may clear to allow their light to shine more brightly. The origins of Christianity are of great historical interest, but this investigation also has been part of a lifelong quest to understand vital truths that have guided my life. As a young Christian I discovered that the Bible was not perfect, but the certainty I had sought in a book never really existed in the first place.

Truly, we know only in part, and we see only a dim reflection, as Paul wrote so poetically (1 Cor. 13:12). The heart of love I had found remained as vital as ever, and I saw new meaning in the words of Jesus, that "the truth will make you free."

Bibliography

Barrett, C.K. *The New Testament Background*. San Francisco: Harper, 1995.

Borg, Marcus J. *Meeting Jesus Again for the First Time*. New York: Harper One, 1994.

Brown, Dan. *The Da Vinci Code*. Doubleday, 2003.

Cartlidge, David R., and David L. Dungan, eds. *Documents for the Study of the Gospels*. Minneapolis: Fortress, 1994.

Caruso, Steve. *Problems with Peshitta Primacy*. The Aramaic New Testament: Galilean Aramaic in the Context of Early Christianity, 2012, <http://aramaicnt.org/articles/problems-with-peshitta-primacy/#return-note-325-1>

Crossan, John Dominic. *The Historical Jesus: The Life of a Mediterranean Jewish Peasant*. San Francisco: Harper San Francisco, 1991.

————. *Jesus, a Revolutionary Biography*. San Francisco: Harper San Francisco, 1994.

Crossan, John Dominic, and Jonathan L. Reed. *Excavating Jesus: Beneath the Stones, Behind the Texts*. San Francisco: Harper San Francisco, 2001.

Drake, H.A. *Constantine and the Bishops: Politics of Intolerance*. John Hopkins, 2000.

Ehrman, Bart D. *After the New Testament: A Reader in Early Christianity*. New York: Oxford University Press, 1999.

————. *Jesus: Apocalyptic Prophet of the New Millennium*. New York: Oxford University Press, 1999.

————. *Lost Christianities: The Battles for Scripture and the Faiths We Never Knew*. New York: Oxford University Press, 2003.

————. *Lost Scriptures: Books That Did Not Make It into the New Testament*. New York: Oxford University Press, 2003.

————. *Misquoting Jesus: The Story Behind Who Changed the Bible and Why*. San Francisco: Harper San Francisco, 2005.

————. *The New Testament: A Historical Introduction to the Early Christian Writings*. 3rd ed. New York: Oxford University Press, 2004.

————. *The Orthodox Corruption of Scripture: The Effect of Early Christological Controversies on the Text of the New Testament*. New York: Oxford University Press, 1993.

Funk, Robert W., Roy W. Hoover, and The Jesus Seminar. *The Five Gospels: The Search for the Authentic Words of Jesus*. New York: MacMillan, 1993.

Goldberg, G.J. *The Flavius Josephus Home Page*. Josephus.org website, 2010. http://josephus.org.

Gurtner, Daniel M. *The Gospel of Mark in Syriac Christianity*. Paper presented at the SBL Annual Meeting (Baltimore, 2013) in the Syriac Literature and Interpretations of Sacred Texts Section, 2013. http://www.academia.edu/3073142/_The_Gospel_of_Mark_in_Syriac_Christianity.

Harris, Stephen L. *The New Testament: A Student's Introduction*. 3rd ed. Mountain View: Mayfield, 1999.

Jensen, Robin M. "How Pilate Became a Saint." *Biblical Review* 19, no. 6 (Dec 2003): Biblical Archaeology Society Online Archive, BASarchive.org. http://www.basarchive.org/sample/bswbBrowse.asp?PubID=BSBR&Volume=19&Issue=6&ArticleID=2.

Johnson, Luke Timothy. *The Real Jesus: The Misguided Quest for the Historical Jesus and the Truth of the Traditional Gospels*. San Francisco: Harper San Francisco, 1996.

King, Karen L. *The Gospel of Mary of Magdala: Jesus and the First Woman Apostle*. Santa Rosa: Polebridge, 2003.

Kirby, Peter. *Early Christian Writings*. Website, 2015. http://www.earlychristianwritings.com.

———. *Early Jewish Writings*. Website, 2015. http://www.earlyjewishwritings.com.

Koester, Helmut. *Ancient Christian Gospels: Their History and Development*. Harrisburg: Trinity, 1990.

LaHaye, T., and J.B. Jenkins. *Left Behind*. Tyndale House, 1995.

Levine, Amy-Jill. *The Misunderstood Jew: The Church and the Scandal of the Jewish Jesus*. San Francisco: Harper San Francisco, 2006.

Levine, Amy-Jill, Dale. C. Allison Jr., and John Dominic Crossan, eds. *The Historical Jesus in Context*: Princeton University Press, 2006.

Levine, Amy-Jill, and Marc Zvi Brettler. *The Jewish Annotated New Testament*. New York: Oxford University Press, 2011.

Lewis, C.S. *The World's Last Night and Other Essays*. Harcourt, 1960.

Lindsey, Hal, and Carole C. Carlson. *The Late Great Planet Earth*. Zondervan, 1970.

Meyer, Marvin W. *The Gospels of Mary: The Secret Tradition of Mary Magdalene the Companion of Jesus*. San Franciso: Harper San Francisco, 2004.

———. *The Secret Teachings of Jesus: Four Gnostic Gospels*. New York: Vintage, 1984.

Newsome, James D. *Greeks, Romans, Jews: Currents of Belief and Culture in the New Testament World*. Philadelphia: Trinity International, 1992.

Oral Roberts University. *Join Oref*. ORUEF website, 2015. http://www.oru.edu/academics/resources/new_oruef/membership/join_oruef.php

Pagels, Elaine. *Adam and Eve and the Serpent*. New York: Vintage, Random House, 1988.

———. *Beyond Belief: The Secret Gospel of Thomas*. New York: Random House, 2003.

———. *The Gnostic Gospels*. New York: Random House, 1979.

Pagels, Elaine, and Karen L. King. *Reading Judas: The Gospel of Judas and the Shaping of Christianity*. New York: Viking/Penguin, 2007.

Robinson, James M., ed. *The Nag Hammadi Library*. New York: Harper Collins, 1990.

Rubenstein, Richard E. *When Jesus Became God: The Struggle to Define Christianity During the Last Days of Rome*. Harcourt, 1999.

Sanders, E.P. *The Historical Figure of Jesus*. London: Allen Lane/Penguin, 1993.

Schaff, Phillip. *Creeds of Christendom, with a History and Critical Notes. Volume I*. Harper & Brothers, 1877.

Schiffman, Lawrence H. *Qumran and Jerusalem: Studies in the Dead Sea Scrolls and the History of Judaism.* Grand Rapids: Eerdmans, 2010.

———. *Reclaiming the Dead Sea Scrolls: Their True Meaning for Judaism and Christianity.* New Haven: Yale University Press, 1994.

———. *Understanding Second Temple and Rabbinic Judaism.* Jersey City: Ktav, 2003.

Southern Baptist Convention. *Basic Beliefs.* Sbc.net website, 2015. http://www.sbc.net/aboutus/basicbeliefs.asp

VanderKam, James C. *An Introduction to Early Judaism.* Grand Rapids: Eerdmans, 2001.

Whiston, William. *Josephus: The Complete Works, Translated by William Whiston, A.M.* Nashville: Thomas Nelson, 1998.

Index